ROLES OF TRADITIONAL AUTHORITY LEADERS

in *Taking Towns to Rural Peoples*
in the Republic of South Sudan

ROLES OF TRADITIONAL AUTHORITY LEADERS

in *Taking Towns to Rural Peoples* in the Republic of South Sudan

Acuil Malith Banggol

Africa
World Books
Pty Ltd

Published by
Africa World Books

Published by Africa World Books, Perth, Australia
Edited by Catherine Schwerin

Roles of Traditional Authority Leaders in *Taking Towns to Rural Peoples* in the Republic of South Sudan

Copyright © 2017
ISBN: 978-0-9876141-1-7

Disclaimers

Readers and users of any information included in this book *The Roles of Traditional Authority Leaders in Taking Towns to Rural Peoples in South Sudan* are advised to seek up-to-date, accurate and/or complete information. Readers and users of any information contained herein are responsible for identifying and avoiding any misleading expression or misrepresentation of this content. The purpose of this publication is to encourage interested communities, entities and/or individuals to engage collaboratively in mutual recognition and dialogue for the sake of harmony and peaceful coexistence amongst the peoples of South Sudan.

The information and views set out in this publication are solely those of the author and do not necessarily reflect the opinions of the publishers. Neither the publishers nor any person acting on their behalf may be held responsible for the nature, veracity or accuracy of the information contained herein or the use which may be made thereof.

DEDICATION

To you, my brother Ustaz J. Aguek Malith Banggol, you envisioned, you educated me!

And to the passionate nationalist and martyr *Gbia* (P/Chief) and founding Chairman of Western Bahr Ghazal State Council of Traditional Authority Leaders (COTAL), Angelo Bagari Umgbanga UKOVO. He was assassinated on 10 May 2015 at his home in his newly founded Bagari County Headquarters of Western Bahr El Ghazal State. *Gbia* Angelo Bagari courageously envisioned an inclusive future for our country and paid the ultimate price to see his vision come true. UKOVO! Your revolutionary vision of *Taking Towns to Rural Peoples* in South Sudan is attainable!

TABLE OF CONTENTS

TABLE OF FIGURES

TABLE OF DIAGRAMS

ACKNOWLEDGEMENTS

I am gratefully indebted to the supervisor of this study, Dr Abednego Akok Kacuol, for his unwavering commitment in providing the necessary corrections, suggestions and coaching. Thanks is also due to Catherine Schwerin for her editorial skills and her commitment to this publication. My distinct gratitude is owed to the Government of Switzerland and Gurtong Magazine for sponsoring my trip to and from Ghana, South Africa and Botswana. The tour enabled me to learn about the legacy and status of Traditional Authority Leaders and their role in people-centred, interactive, participatory and inclusive good governance in the countries visited.

Particular appreciation is due to Dr Chris Jones-Pulley, a lawyer who engaged with the level of my language style and expression. She provided consistent back-up support throughout the process of conceptualisation, design and information gathering on this study. I am beholden to the inspirational influence of Dr Conradin Perner (Kwacakworo), Dr Alfred Lokuji, Jacob J. Akol and Christina Jones-Pauly. They laboured to cogwheel a sense of inclusivity in me. Individual thanks go to Martina Santschi, a researcher, and Sophia Dawkins for precious literature and intellectual stimulation. Thanks go to Josef Bucher for his encouragement. He instilled in me a sense of enthusiasm and helped me communicate my views in this regard.

My heartfelt thanks goes to Ms Achol Jok Mac and Augustino Ting for their sustained support. They helped me come out of my personal, complex views, as well as with the language and required procedures of the research and presentation style. Thanks to Apuk Ayuel for taking notes during discussions. Special appreciation is due to Humble Oliver for contributing the photos used in this report. Computer wizard Ambassador Thiik Agoth Giirdit kept a watch on my fingers; my friends Mawan Gordon Muortat and Ms Sylvia Njuguna helped me with a head-torch and dry cells from London and Nairobi. The head spotlights and dry cells were precious and enabling factors to me where there was no electricity.

Special appreciation is due to the International Leadership Institute family, in particular the charismatic and visionary Professor Badeg, Dr Girma Gezahegn and Mr David Ruach Tong, who intellectually, emotionally, spiritually and physically transformed me and my colleagues during our course and assignments. Thanks to Dr Ann Itto, Deputy Secretary General of the SPLM. She granted fundamental support by spontaneously approving my movements, which could not have yielded fruit without kind support and repeated unlimited permissions to attend to my varied assignments. I would also like to give special thanks to the outstanding South Sudanese philanthropist and visionary businessman Cde Makiir Gai Thiep, the Aguok Community Leader, for providing financial support to meet publication costs.

Finally, this work was made possible and pleasant because my dear wife Akec, my relatives and children Awak-aguentung and Ringmanam gave me a sweet home in our house. Phone calls from my daughter Aluk were soothing and inspiring.

Thank you all! You, all, inspired and furnished me abundantly.

ACRONYMS

ARCISS   Agreement on the Resolution of the Conflict in South Sudan

COTAL   Council of Traditional Authority Leaders

CPA   Comprehensive Peace Agreement

GoSS   Government of South Sudan

HoN   House of Nationalities

IDEG   Institute for Democratic Governance

IRI   International Republican Institute

LGA   Local Government Act

LGB   Local Government Board

MoFA   Ministry of Federal Affairs

NBS   National Bureau of Statistics

NCP   National Congress Party

PASS   Policy Advocacy & Strategic Studies

RSS   Republic of South Sudan

SPLA   Sudan People's Liberation Army

SPLM   Sudan People's Liberation Movement

TAL   Traditional Authority Leader/Leadership

TCFS   Traditional Communal Federal System

TGoNU   Transitional Government of National Unity

CHAPTER ONE:
INTRODUCTION AND BACKGROUND
TO THE STUDY

Introduction to the study

This study was conducted in 2013/14 in the Republic of South Sudan on the anticipated roles that could be played by traditional authority leaders (TALs) to sustainably, and in a timely fashion, enhance efforts in realising the goal of the project *Taking Towns to Rural Peoples*. The research aimed at expounding upon the meaning and purpose of this policy of *Taking Towns to Rural Peoples*.

The hypothesis of this research was that the most efficient methods for implementing this policy could be through the recognition and incorporation of TAL institutions and the related Councils of Traditional Authority Leaders (COTALs) as mandated by political will, policy outlook and the law. The purpose of this research was to examine the assertion that an 'organizational culture' (Peggy 1997: 4) of twining could be institutionalised by ways and means of weaving the modern political nation-state on the one hand with the traditional communal federal systems (TCFSs) of governance under several community-enthroned TALs on the other (Model 1 in Chapter 6). This envisioned model of twining could be achieved by recognising the status and roles of traditional authority leadership institutions (TAL institutions) and by subsequently fulfilling a legal framework mandating the incorporation of TAL institutions in the establishment, composition and functions of the modern political nation-state of the executive and legislature at the national, state and local government levels in the country.

The significance of this presupposition is based on a hypothesis of this research that perceives South Sudan as a social, political, economic, cultural and administrative establishment whose level of success in the public administration is tied to accomplishing the incorporation of TALs and TCFSs as mandated under article 166, 167, 168 and 169 of South Sudan Transitional Constitution (SSTC) 2011. In that, in South Sudan, each of the TCFSs – a chieftain or a kingdom – is perceived and exists as the traditional customary communal homeland to each and/or several chieftains of the 72 nationalities, estimated to be thousands of culturally discrete communities with reciprocal mutual recognition and a desire to coexist peacefully. Each homeland and society is ascribed with discrete patterns of diverse livelihoods, practices, norms and distinct cultural values. The term 'federation' was avoided for tactical reasons during negotiations leading to the Comprehensive Peace Agreement (CPA) in 2005. The then liberation movement and now a ruling party, the Sudan People's Liberation Movement (SPLM), favoured the term 'decentralisation'. The party consistently maintained its envisioned decentralisation at the SPLM 2008 Party Convention. But the notion of federalisation is explicitly mandated under paragraph IV.11 of SPLM Manifesto 2008 as: '… a decentralized power structure with a view to devolving more **federal** powers to the regions and, where and when necessary, full autonomy…' (my emphasis).

Public Administration – the traditional governance system – and sociopolitical perceptions and patterns of TAL institutions in South Sudan are practised in form and content such that each subnationality or subsection is ascribed to a communal public administration that could be termed as a societal nationhood or a state – *wut* in Dinka or a clan in English – as a traditional, customary, communal federal administration unit that identifies itself distinctively within itself and with respect to other communities. As such, each TAL institution is identified as a commune with territorial integrity. Perceived communally, it is understood and professed, but observed, respected and protected with rights restricted by mutual customary laws. These include rights to build dwellings, conduct burials, create shrines for worship, and compose sentimental and emphatic praise songs of belonging to the homeland. These songs usually include praise of self-exultation and efficacy, right to cultivation, fishing, grazing of livestock, and hunting. These rights include sustainable exploitation and management of forest products while hosting others for mutual coexistence upon approval and ritualistically allowed by the elders of the society. A citizen and community group would demonstrate decent desire to sacrifice and devote life and property to contribute towards protection and mutual dependence within the society.

On 9 July 2011, the Republic of South Sudan was founded as a sovereign, modern, political nation-state that had been moulded by a history of struggle and emphatic mutuality. Under each TCFS – *wut* in Dinka, *cheng* in Nuer and *kal* in Chollo, for example – the rights and values enjoyed under traditional communal

3

federations have inevitably rekindled and continued to create the bonds and fabric manifested in social contracts of kin and kith. This connectedness could be explained in the political, economic and cultural identity of a cohesive customary communal livelihood. Such coexistence in each commune is obviously vital and is positively identical to and noticeably discrete from its neighbouring communes. Each of such communities exists now in the form and content of customary communal social desire and a general will. This societal desire accommodates individual desires to freely choose not to contravene the commune and a South Sudanese general will for liberty and mutuality. This manifestation of South Sudanese commonality and the general will was demonstrated through the record high and overwhelming, yet credible, vote of 98.83% for independence in the results of the historic 2011 referendum. Ensuring sustainable freedom, peace and prosperity requires unity in diversity founded on mutual recognition and respect for all by all. This could guarantee sustainable peaceful coexistence, mutuality and prosperity for all, irrespective of gender, faith, nationality and social strata. Incorporating and institutionalising these values, norms and practices in the modern nation-state could enhance mutual social cohesion.

For centuries in South Sudan, these cohesions sprang from a sense of identity as a self-styled societal nation-state with communal collectiveness protected by legions of age-sets (groups) of *Rich Rem* in Dinka, *Monyomiji* in Ottuhu and *Buulok* in Murle, for example. Though such TCFSs lacked the modern perception of sovereignty recognised internationally by the United Nations and did not operate diplomatic connectivity and international treaties similar to the modern political nation-state, TCFSs served as viable units of the wholesomeness of South Sudanese commonality and nationhood. Each distinct communal governance as a TCFS under a TAL identified with a recognised livelihood and mutuality that has and shall continue to serve to cement unity in diversity in South Sudan. It seems problematic and utopian to blindly opt to assimilate through an archaic call for 'one people'. This notion tends to ignore cultural diversity by misidentifying it as a challenge to commonality. Assimilation is not only against liberty and opposed to nature, but researchers on communality (Koller et al. 2012: 17–18) have identified evidence that all attempts to ignore differences have ended up in disharmony. Under all the forced unity there is a fierce resistance, social unrest, racial discrimination, and chronic political instability and insecurity. Hence unity in diversity is the preferred goal.

The tragedy, blamed on the apparent demonisation of TCFSs, is that the sociopolitical and cultural practices, human resources and natural wealth of TCFSs became the target of destruction and looting by the invading colonisers. This was later institutionalised through the 1884 Berlin Conference, dubbed the Scramble for Africa. At this conference, the colonisers imposed the forms and contents of their exotic exploitative, exclusive and oppressive political nation-states, which continued to demonise TCFSs and TALs. The sentiment 'local' is suspected to have evolved from the superiority mentality that was justified by the then derived ethnicity theory.

The theory was founded on the sociopolitical assimilation model established on the racial connotation of 'white race superiority' over other races. This ethnicity theory, put forth in the 1920s by sociologist Robert E. Park, was based on the notion of the superiority of white culture. This crude theory in turn was founded on another imprudent biological essentialist theory that bred perceptions of savagery, barbarity and ethnicity against trends towards nationhood. Since then the term 'ethnicity' has been used to justify cultural monism. Cultural monism rejects 'unity in diversity'. Monism considers unity in diversity as an obstacle to assimilation to a monocultural singularity. It tends to endorse the dominance of a 'superior' culture. Its history is shown and is manifested in apartheid, fascism, ultraisms, and now religious and racial intolerance and extremism. In South Sudan, this could be blamed for innocent sectionism, sexism, social guruism and 'tribalism' threatening modernity and unity in diversity in multicultural and multinational South Sudan. The ethnicity theory of monism is baselessly founded on the erroneous perception that those who do not try to hang onto the 'superior' culture by accepting assimilation are responsible for remaining inferior, and as such may be identified as an 'ethnic group'. It is on the basis of this naïve theory that religious believers with a feudalistic outlook irrationally endorsed slavery and used it to justify ownership of slaves from enslaved 'ethnicities'. The other obvious reason for choosing the label 'local' was to demonise community-enthroned chiefs, kings, and queens and by extension, the presidents or heads of the colonised states and to belittle the colonised nationalities – the TCFSs and their TALs. Thus it is likely that this is why the word 'local' authority was chosen. But for the purpose of clarity, the word is adopted here as 'traditional' or communal to mean originally from the lifestyle of the South Sudanese peoples' nationalities.

The TCFS is a description of a traditional societal nation-state under a traditionally enthroned authority and its leadership, commonly referred to as traditional authority leaders (TALs). In this, each nationality may be made up of many major subnationalities. For example, the Dinka nationality is made up of Rek and Padang. Each of these is further subdivided into a subgroup composed of a TCFS (*wut*) in South Sudan. Each TCFS coexists within itself and with other TCFSs, resulting in what this study terms as a customary TCFS, with customary governance and a public administration. A TCFS is characterised by autonomous traditional governance and mutual coexistence within itself and with neighbouring traditional communes' systems of governance. To reiterate, this TCFS is founded on values of mutuality, good neighbourliness and unity in diversity as a sustainable peaceful coexistence and affinity.

Diversity in cultures and models of livelihood notwithstanding, in political terms the South–South collaborative resistance evolved before and after 658–664 AD, with the invasion of an exclusive theocratic nation-state headed by Amr ibn al-'Aas. This invasion period is marked by the encroachment of the fascistic and theocratic Arabised system of subjugation and exploitative governance (Igga: 2010). This was the start of ensuing invasions by other colonisers, like the Turks in 1821 (Yom: 2008, Malok: 2009 and Arop: 2012). This was followed by the 1884 Berlin Conference, which divided African territories up according to perceived colonial rights to annex African lands, enslave its citizens, destroy its societies and pillage its resources. In their research, Malok (2009) and Arop (2012) each suggested evidence indicating that resistance by leadership and institutions of TALs enhanced the liberation process in 1955–1972 and 1983–2004 (Kuol: 2008), which ultimately led to the achievement of sovereignty on 9 July 2011. TAL institutions were recognised, and they effectively linked colonial administration with colonised communities (Malok: 2009). TALs helped link rural livelihoods with rudimentary administration of justice and social service programs initiated by the colonisers.

TAL institutions remained relevant in the modern political nation-state of South Sudan. But this freed modern political nation-state of South Sudan seems to neglect the huge potentials of its TALs. As a suspected spillover from colonisers, the liberated political nation-state is mistakenly deepening the process that tends to demonise the roles played by TALs. This is occurring despite the obvious reality that the nascent nation-state institutions are weak. They are characterised by limited capacities, poor access and, as a result, insignificant presence in rural areas.

In envisioning a solution to this disreputable anomaly, comrade President Kiir in a historic address on the occasion of the Oath of the Justice of the Supreme Court, on 3 June 2006, reminded everyone that:

> ...Our governance must be well grounded in
> our traditional laws and customs... It must be

borne in mind by all that this has been one of the underlying causes in the quest for freedom and human dignity. Our culture identification and development in all its forms must be unchained and facilitated to reach the same heights, as is the case elsewhere in our continent or the rest of the globe for that matter...

These notions of inclusivity are legitimised by SSTC 2011, articles 2, 33, 36(4), 37, 166, 167, 168, 169(3) of SSTC 2011 and specifically 166(6)(b) and (c) mandating to 'establish the local government institutions as close as possible to the people' and 'encourage the involvement of communities and community based organizations in all matters of local government, and promote dialogue among them on matters of local interest'.

Correspondingly, following the same political outlook, the SPLM Constitution 2008 under article 5(8), which calls for diversity, mandates: 'Justice and equality for all irrespective of ethnicity [nationality], religion, region, social status or gender'. It underlines unity in diversity. With respect to diversity under article 5(10), the SPLM Constitution 2008 mandates respect for cultural heritage, values and beliefs. Explicitly on governance under paragraph IV.11 of the SPLM Manifesto 2008, the policy expounds on decentralisation with '...a view to devolving more federal powers to the regions and, where and when necessary, full autonomy...'

Background to the study

...The demands of security, which is an indispensable pre-requisite to keeping the CPA 2015 on track, have deprived us of the financial resources required to expedite the process of translating the goal of Taking Towns to Rural Areas into concrete reality... Government officers who do not know enough to know that our real wealth is in the renewable natural resources of South Sudan: land, water and forests and in the industry of our people: farmers, herdsmen and fishermen, shall have a short life in my government...
(President Kiir, 21 May 2010)

With progress in implementation of the CPA 2005 and successful conduct of the General Consensus in 2008 through support by TALs, the president of the then Government of Southern Sudan, Comrade Kiir, envisioned and directed the conference of Southern Sudan All Kings, Chiefs and Traditional Authority Leaders in Bentiu, 18–22 May 2009. This collaborative dialogue proved vital. The conference helped to diagnose challenges and allowed collaborative dialogue and successful mobilisation of communities and the TALs for a common purpose. The direct positive impact was a firm support to implementation of the CPA 2005. Above all the conference contributed in achieving the record high, near-unanimous 98.83% vote for separation of South Sudan on 9 January 2011. Furthermore, in his inaugural speech after winning the 2010 General Elections as President of the Government of Southern

Sudan, President Kiir on 21 May 2010 acknowledged the roles of TALs:

>...Traditional leaders, law-enforcement agencies and the communities at large stood firm against the fomenters of trouble. In this respect, they have shown the same resilience, which they have exhibited during the struggle to thwart all attempts to divide them or disturb peace and disrupt tranquillity in their communities. I would also like to applaud their cooperation during the disarmament and I take this opportunity to inform you of the government efforts to collect light arms from the population as per CPA provisions...

President Kiir declared that:

>...The Government of Southern Sudan shall continue to provide our traditional leaders with all the support and means they need to ensure peace in their communities. It shall guarantee that our regular forces are furnished with the best training; tools and equipment that shall enable them carry out their scared duty...

The point of departure of this study assumes that, in South Sudan, a quick assessment of the reasons why implementation of this popular goal of *Taking Towns to Rural Peoples* is held back suggests that lack of adherence to mandated policies on TALs is to be blamed. These policies explicitly mandate recognition of status and involvement of TAL institutions as mandated by SSTC 2011 and the Local Government Act (LGA) 2009. However, it is also noticeable that a weak institutional framework persists and that organisational cultures have not been established to fulfil the mandates of section 12(b) of LGA 2009. This provision mandates that the government should establish the local government institutions as close as possible to the people. Provisions of article 166(6)(c) call for the involvement of communities and community-based organisations in local government and promoting dialogue amongst them on matters of local interest. TCFSs – kingdoms and chieftaincies under TALs – are the closest.

Logically, it could be suspected that implementation of the goal of *Taking Towns to Rural Peoples* is lagging because of inadequate adherence to LGA 2009 section 19(3) mandating the *boma* to be the main domain of the TALs. It is at that level that TALs could perform their administrative and customary duties. Its implementation is further impeded due to lack of adherence to SSTC 2011 article 169(3), mandating the national government to promote and encourage the participation of the people – the communities – in the formulation of national policies on development and programs. The negative results of such impediments are exacerbated by inconsistence in competence associated with inconsistence of SSTC 2011 articles 50 through to 59 on the establishment, composition and functions of the executive and the legislature at national, state and local government levels. These provisions contravene the spirit of articles 47, 48, 49 of SSTC 2011, which mandate a decentralised system with regard to levels of government, devolution of powers and intergovern-mental linkage respectively. These inconsistencies are also evidently to be noted in non-adherence to articles 166, 167, 168 and 169(3) of SSTC 2011 on mandated recognition of status, roles, functions and involvement of TAL systems in the composition, establishment and functions of national and state governments.

The consequence is that rural communities have not enjoyed involvement in policy formulation and implementation as explicitly mandated by LGA 2009 and SSTC 2011. Such roles have been taken over by the elites, who bear contempt for traditional communities. Elites treat rural communities in the same manner as the colonial invaders and masters did during the periods 1821–1955 and 1956–2005. In these periods, the colonisers' interest was in centralised power and authority exercised by the privileged elites, who excluded rural communities and their traditional systems of governance from major decision-making and policymaking processes. The colonisers exploited the status of TALs for the purposes of mobilising rural communities to provide the colonisers with resources like minerals, elephant tusk, ostrich feathers, slaves and labour. Under colonisation, rural peoples were not deemed worthy of respect, but were only a target of subjugation under colonial rules.

Contrary to the claim that the colonisers established the TALs, evidence is clear that TALs and TCFSs existed even prior to the 19th century. TALs were instrumental in mobilising their communities to defend against slavery, annexation of their land, destruction and looting of properties (Malok 2009: 4–5 and Arop 2012: 1–17). Sources pertaining to Sudan speak of King Pianki (Lual: 2003). The Bible mentions the ancient Kingdom of Morwe, amongst others. Even after conceding to colonial forces, TALs were recognised and incorporated by colonial administrations. TALs served as connectors to the rural community. That incorporation was for the purposes of governance, administration of justice, building roads and schools, and enrolment of children for education (Arop 2012: 5–7). Later on, TALs played a pivotal role in shaping the struggle of the peoples of South Sudan against marginalisation and exclusion by Khartoum during the period from 1947 to 1955 (Malok 2009: 17–50). TALs dominated the ability to support livelihoods and governance in the rural areas, which in turn enhanced the role of the liberation struggle during the period 1955–2004 (Kuol 2008: 69–83). It was clear that TALs were pivotal in efforts to achieve the 98.83% vote for independence in 2011.

According to Wassara (2007: 8), traditionally, preservation of culture and adherence to common laws, values and informal economic transaction and resolution of disputes arising in implementation of such acquaintances amongst the rural communities are critical aspects of the role that TALs play in South Sudan. This researcher has extensively engaged TALs, like many other peace promoters who now engage them. TAL institutions play a clearly significant role in enhancing negotiation amongst warring communities or in dialogue for peaceful coexistence, and mutuality in using shared natural resources. TALs have been instrumental in the essential people-to-people peace process. Therefore, it is reasonable to assume that the TAL system could play an important role in mobilising rural peoples to realise and widely own the goals of *Taking Towns to Rural Peoples in South Sudan.*

Since 2003 and after proclamation of independence on 9 July 2011, *Taking Towns to Rural Peoples,* as a favourable political will, envisioned recognition and involvement of TALs and COTALs. The policy rested on a premise that represented the opposite to the previous colonial mentality of invaders, whether under the Anglo-Egyptian Condominium colonial rule from 1885 to 1955 or under exclusive policies of Old Sudan under Khartoum (Malok 2010 and Arop 2011). The policy as a peace dividend is evidently deeply indebted to the constitutional provisions of the Interim Constitution of Southern Sudan 2005, now carried over into the current SSTC 2011. The constitutional underpinnings that mandate TAL systems being incorporated as an integral part of the proposed routinised forums (Chapter 4) should be highlighted. It is assumed that if these collaborative and inclusive routinised forums are instituted, recognised and involved, it could enhance the process to complement the roles of the executive and legislature in realising inclusive good governance and an effective 'leadership molecule' (Flamholtz and Randle 2008: 60) at national, state and local governments levels.

Taking Towns to Rural Peoples, as a social and political endeavour, is aimed at devolving more federal powers by bringing decision-making processes and decisions to lower administrative units in *boma* and closer to communities, so as to intensify access to basic social services and thus attain improved quality of life amongst rural communities. It is intended to curb undesirable rural–urban migration of youth. Controllable yet ill-guided education is creating a process of spiral growth of jobseekers from the inelastic public administration in government. The ill-guided system of education is injecting bad habits into unskilled immigrant rural youth who have become vulnerable and jobless in urban centres. Rural immigrants are then exposed to antisocial behaviours in those urban areas. Moreover, rural–urban migration impedes rural youth responsibilities in food production, thus heightening food insecurity in rural areas caused by lack of sufficient numbers in the agricultural labour force. Evidence has shown that egoistic politicians, for the purpose of pressurising for political jobs, are increasingly exploiting the apathy and vulnerability of this ever-spiralling social stratum. The solution is *Taking Towns to Rural Peoples*.

Good intentions, political will and legal provisions, however, need to be translated into concrete action supported by an institutional framework, organisational culture and a collaborative 'leadership molecule' (Flamholtz and Randle 2008: 60). This leadership molecule should constructively recognise roles and involve all actors and their leadership in matters of their interests. Up to now, the idea of the participation of TALs in governance structures and the policy of *Taking Towns to Rural Peoples* has attracted mammoth attention, even in the media. The predicament is that it is bound with anxiety and with possible negative agitation at national and state level in the country, as well as at local levels, because there has been no progress so far.

Most of the ten states have enacted the draft of the COTAL Bill 2011, in compliance with SSTC 2011 and their State Transitional Constitutions 2011. However, unexpectedly, no single state has practically transformed a COTAL Act 2011 into reframed institutions and the envisioned development culture (Simonsen 1997: 56). Involvement of communities and community-based institutions in matters that influence them is enshrined under article 166(6)(c) of SSTC 2011, but there is no evidence that the executive and the legislature have adhered to it. This exclusionary tendency is not in compliance with any of the State Transitional Constitutions 2011 or the Local Government Act (LGA) 2009. Consequentially, TAL institutions and their benefactors, namely the rural population, are bewildered, puzzled and mystified in finding remedies to such exclusion and marginalisation. Such exclusion is evident from the level of national budget allocation during 2006 to 2011. The national budget consumed 74% of the resources, while only 26% was reserved for all the ten states (Deng 2013: 50). There was no evidence of any allocation to rural areas throughout South Sudan. No level of executive and legislature has so far adhered to the mandate of articles 167 and 168 on the establishment and recognition of COTALs at state and national levels.

Statement of the research problem

The literature review revealed that constitutional provisions on the establishment, composition and functions of national, state and local governments in the Republic of South Sudan are inconsistent with constitutional mandates under article 2 on sovereignty vested on the peoples' will. They do not match the expressed values of article 35 of the SSTC on the guiding principles of governance, 36 on political goals, 37 on economic goals, or 47 on mandated levels of government that include TALs. Similarly, it is noted that the provisions of article 48 on the devolution of powers and article 49 on intergovernmental linkage are explicit about respecting the powers of others and not encroaching on mandated powers. Additionally, provisions under articles 50 and beyond on the establishment, composition and functions of the executive and legislature at national and state levels are compatible with the provisions of articles 167, 168, 169 on the status, roles and recognition of TAL institutions and their COTALs at national and state levels of government.

This unconstitutional exclusion, disfranchisement and marginalisation of rural peoples and their TAL institutions inhibits their involvement in decisions on matters that affect them as mandated by article 166(6)(c) of SSTC 2011. Such marginalisation of TALs could be claimed to inhibit rural dwellers' chance to enjoy the dividends of peace envisaged in the policy of *Taking Towns to Rural Peoples*. Subsequently, in realisation of *Taking Towns to Rural Peoples*, relegation of the roles of TAL institutions has rendered unexplored a legacy of TALs and their demonstrated transformational leadership and change characteristics (Bass and Riggio, 2006: 21).

To paraphrase Zaninotto (2011: 15–19), South Sudan is a country that needs social building involving nationalities (and their TALs), which are faced with the challenges of sharing national resources and the resultant competition within and amongst each other. The challenge is that the ruling elites tend to demonise and exclude these nationalities and their TAL institutions. The unconstitutional tendency of elites to exclude and to hinder the recognition, involvement and incorporation of TALs in public administration hinders the opportunity to create the needed network, discourse and mutuality envisioned for peaceful coexistence. Such unity in diversity could enhance the creation of a South Sudanese commonality and a multicultural nationhood. Exclusion of TAL institutions inhibits their role as the human factor essential to empowering weak government institutions in governance and an organisational culture that could be pivotal in the delivery of services. The consequence of this exclusion is a rampant loss of resources along the unconstitutionally centralised system between states and local government. It limits the abilities of TALs and TCFSs to mobilise the rural majority to be peaceful and self-reliant. It could be contended that it is this undermining of TALs and TCFSs that is causing implementation of the goal of *Taking Towns to Rural Peoples* to be retarded and impeded in the Republic of South Sudan.

Research question

The basic question being asked is this: Is this undermining of TAL institutions and their exclusion in all levels of government in South Sudan deliberate by design or is it a policy oversight or a mere curse of cluelessness about existing constitutional mandates on TAL and related COTAL institutions?

This basic question is subdivided into four questions:

1. What led to the lack of recognition of the status and roles of TAL institutions, which undermines the mandated process to recognise the status and to involve TAL institutions in the establishment, composition and functions of legislature and executive at national, state and local government levels?

2. Could effective recognition and involvement of TAL institutions and their transformational leadership and change characteristics in decision-making processes and mobilisation expedite realisation of the desired future state (Simonson 1997: 54) of *Taking Towns to Rural Peoples?*

3. What legal provisions and reframed institutional structures could be suggested to make the legislature and executive in national, state and local government mandatorily engage TAL institutions and COTALs in envisioned consultative routinised forums?

4. What institutional framework and organisational culture might enhance the role of transformational and change leaders at national levels to engage TAL institutions in dialogue and influence the timely and consistent promotion of the required futuring, networking, collaborative learning, discourse, dialogue and renaissance (Hames 2007: 181–208), and to create a leadership molecule (Flamholtz & Randle 2008: 60) that could enhance inclusivity and the incorporation of TAL institutions in the establishment, composition and functions of the legislature and executive in national, state and local government?

Objectives of the study

The overall objective of this research was to investigate how TALs could be involved in the implementation of the policy of *Taking Town to Rural Peoples*. It also aims to discuss possible ways of helping TAL institutions gain access to consultative forums and an inclusive leadership molecule that could enhance collaborative attainment of the envisioned wellbeing of the rural peoples in South Sudan. Based on the overall objectives, the following specific objectives of the study have been identified:

- Identify empirical evidence of the significance of TAL institutions and COTAL roles in participating in rural development and the sustainable modern political nation-state of South Sudan.
- Review the institutional and legal framework connecting TAL institutions and COTALs on the one hand and the legislature and executive in national, state and local governments on the other.
- Provide recommendations on the legal and institutional frameworks on how to involve TAL institutions in discourse in the national, state and local government executive and legislature, to identify needs and priorities in decision-making, implementation and review of the development policy of *Taking Towns to Rural Peoples.*

Significance of the study

Taking Towns to Rural Peoples is a major concern to rural peoples in South Sudan. Also, political leaders and the media consider it as a solution that will provide improved quality of life and development in rural areas. It is anticipated to be a solution ensuring that resources can reach the rural peoples and that rural peoples can be involved in decisions on matters that affect them.

Findings and recommendations deduced from the findings may promote the required development culture (Simonsen 1997: 56) of weaving and twining between the TCFSs and TALs on the one hand and the political nation-state of South Sudan on the other. The proposed twining may incorporate TAL institutions in the legislature and executive at national, state and local government levels in South Sudan as enshrined in the constitution and an expressed political will. Research anticipates that such a mandate, if enforced, will result in reframing the institutional parameters through the use of routinised forums of COTALs as a complementary and collaborative leadership molecule (Flamholtz and Randle 2008: 60). It is also suspected that the abysmal legal gap has resulted in the further unconstitutional exclusion of TALs and their communities. This exclusion is caused by a combination of possible oversight, cluelessness and/or by design.

Therefore, it is contemplated that this envisioned and desired future state (Peggy 1997: 54) of inclusivity, mutuality and complementary roles of TAL institutions at national and state levels of government is pivotal to realising the goal of and creating South Sudanese commonality. It could revamp a South Sudanese social (Deng 2013:180) and political contract (Deng 2013: 192) between and amongst culturally divided South Sudanese nationalities, the budding nation-state institutions and local governments on the one hand and the TAL systems and their rural communities on the other.

Findings of this research may contribute towards future research on the roles of TAL institutions in creating the needed organisational culture (Simonsen 1997:4) that constitutes good governance as characterised by inclusivity, decentralisation and devolution of powers in South Sudan.

Scope and limitations of the study

First, the scope is limited to investigating the roles and functions of TALs in rural development policy formulation and development. The following were areas covered:

- Collection and analysis of views and perspectives from respondents on the mandated institutional framework defining the roles and functions of TALs and COTALs at local, state and national levels of the legislature, executive and judiciary
- Investigation of current level of participation of TALs in realisation of the policy *Taking Towns to Rural Peoples* in South Sudan
- Feasibility field visits to Ghana, Botswana and South Africa and comparison of lessons learnt from the study tour (see Appendix 10) with interviews of target groups in South Sudan.

There are limitations that had bearings on the study. These included techniques and approaches chosen. A mixture of quantitative and qualitative interviews, field visits and a desk literature review were undertaken. The study employed qualitative research methodology that had some limitations in the findings in that data in the qualitative approach were overloaded. Attempts were made to avoid debatable conclusions to deflect overreaction and conceivable resistance from elites who dominate the public services in South Sudan. Also considered was that the time of research was very short and resources were inadequate. The focus of this research was limited to national government institutions in Juba and Central Equatoria at state level. There was limited access to materials and previous studies conducted to support the study. Poor infrastructure in South Sudan meant that travel to collect necessary data and information was hindered. The level of cooperation of target groups is appreciated. For the purpose of this study, the scope was limited to identifying transformational and change leadership characteristics of TAL roles in realisation of *Taking Town to Rural Peoples.*

Definition and perceptions of terms

Boma: is an administrative unit in the Republic of South Sudan functioning as the first and broadest layer of three tiers of local government (*boma, payam,* county). *Boma* is where the rural majority through their TAL institutions would engage with the political nation-state apparatus of the state administration and national government. *Boma* is legislated under section 19(3) of LGA 2009: 'Boma shall be the main domain of the traditional authority where traditional leaders perform their administration and customary functions'.

Desired future state: Simonson (1997: 54) quoted Beckhard and Harris (1987), who defined the future state

24

as a midway goal between the present state and achievement of the vision. The clearer this goal is, the more support and buy-in a leader will get from the stakeholders – the followers. Leaders should avoid starting with the present to avoid being bogged down in the problem to overcome. A leader is a person who is visionary and able to mobilise towards the goal. It is recommended that transformational and change leaders should define the desired future state.

Peoples: is the plural of a 'people' meaning a community, a nationality or a nation. 'Peoples' is a political term reframed within the SPLM's perception of liberation, which is principled on mutuality and unity in diversity. The expression 'peoples' recognises diversity, equality and inclusivity. The notion of 'peoples' concedes to the status of and identification with a living language of each of the 72 culturally distinct peoples (nationalities) in South Sudan. The essence of the term is persuaded by the compassion, sensitivity, recognition and responsiveness of the visionary founding father of SPLM, Dr Garang, to the then changing contexts and demands locally, regionally and globally. Dr Garang reframed the name suggesting the character of the SPLM to reflect the objective realities of the multicultural status of Old Sudan fuelled with desire for justice and inclusivity. The Sudan Peoples' Liberation Army/Movement, as an identity and a name, considered the need for leadership as a phenomenon of group influence, being mindful of principles of equal status, mutuality, involvement, possession and wider ownership of the liberation process by any and all the marginalised peoples of Sudan. The general will and desire was for a new Sudan within its changing contexts and demands. Logically, the term was coined while cognizant of the significance of the explicit provisions in international human rights laws and the conventions on the rights of various cultural groups – the majority and minorities equally. The term 'peoples' is explicitly mentioned under provisions of the United Nations Charter article 1(2) mandating the purpose of the United Nations. Most importantly the term is mentioned in articles 21(1), 22(1), 23(1) and 24(1) of the African (Banjul) Charter on Human and Peoples' Rights, on rights to existence, liberty to choose mode of livelihood, and the solidarity needed to support the peoples' right to determine their political future. This was mandated to ensure adherence to provisions on the rights of peoples of Southern Sudan to freely exercise their rights to self-determination. These clauses in the international human rights laws hugely influenced the envisioned future state of liberty and freedom of any people or peoples exposed to injustice and exploitation. These provisions satisfied and justified the need for eligible armed struggle and the subsequent demand to exercise their rights to self-determination under these international human rights laws. Again, within the context of this research, the term 'peoples' is revolutionarily distinct and loaded with nuances of justness, mutuality and inclusivity. The use of 'peoples' is a correction to the biased notion of 'tribes' that was used by Khartoum regimes to demonise African Sudanese and to mask the colonial and discriminatory mentality of Khartoum. The abusive word 'tribe' adopted by colonisers was intended to demonise 'other' cultures and languages of African peoples (nationalities) in the country. Khartoum's exclusive principle considered that other nationalities were mere tribes with no languages. Khartoum adopted policies that considered African languages as dialects – *Lahjaat* – of the 'only' Arabic language of the 'only' Arab nationality. In Old Sudan, self-efficacy was demonised as *jahawyia* – connoting backwardness, savageness and repressiveness. The term 'tribe' was adopted to isolate those African peoples and their communities from a perceived 'superior' Arabised 'nationalism' – '*El Gomiyaa El Arabiya*'. In South Sudan, the use of the term 'peoples' within the liberation context has a philosophical, ideological and geopolitical significance, such that each of the 72 nationalities in the liberation process is recognised as a people – *Shaab* – a community, with equal sociopolitical, economic and cultural rights as enshrined in the international human rights laws, for example, the people of Anyuak, the people of Murle and the Dinka people, to mention but a few. Hence SPLM party ideologues use the term 'peoples' in exercise of mutual recognition of all cultures united in diversity.

Political nation-state: The term 'modern political nation-state' is adopted here to refer to the nation-state of the Republic of South Sudan. It is perceived to be a sociopolitical, economic and cultural entity that emerged based on the 1884 Berlin Conference. This infamous forum is popularly known as the Scramble for Africa. The Old Sudan political nation-state was created through this mechanism and became a colony of the feudalistic nation-state of Britain. It took over the Turco-Egyptian portions of Old Sudan and ruled there between 1885 and 1956. The colony was meant to be a source of raw material and a market for finished products

27

manufactured by British factories. The process of colonising Old Sudan created the Sudanese elites. These elites later exploited the 19th century decolonisation move to create a political nation-state that replaced British colonial administration. With imperialistic spillover from the British colonisers, the national elites continued to misidentify the liberated political nation-state and abused it as an oppressive tool to exploit South Sudanese communities via a colonial-like public administration. Like their former masters, the South Sudanese elites have now opted to delegitimise communities, the TCFSs and TALs, while swallowing national wealth and any income through salaries and other benefits to elites.

By 9 July 2011, the modern political nation-state of South Sudan emerged as a result of a community collaboration that resisted delegitimisation by the imperialistic colonial political nation-state out of Khartoum (1955–1972 and 1983–2004). The danger is the suspected tendency of the newly founded modern political nation-state of the Republic of South Sudan to become a prototype imperialistic political nation-state as bad as or worse than the elitist and imperialistic political nation-state that excluded and marginalised the peoples of South Sudan. It is unfortunate that despite explicit political will and the constitutional mandate on recognition, inclusion and involvement of TAL institutions and TCFSs, the predominantly elitist South Sudan seems to be replicating the former colonial nation-state of Khartoum.

Traditional communal federal system (TCFS): Within the context of this study, the term TCFS is used to identify and rephrase a type of sociopolitical, economic and cultural existence and governance before, during and after colonisation. TCFS embodies a perception of a desire to achieve a future state full of passion, mutuality, inclusivity and justice. The TCFS, though not stated in previous studies, continues to exist in the form of chiefdom or kingdom or *wut*. The TCFS is the most viable system even now in the postcolonial epoch. This view is influenced by a perception of the existing sociopolitical, economic and cultural demographic set-up in *boma* administrative units in South Sudan. Within this, in South Sudan, TCFS is a term describing a collaboration of homelands of each of the 72 nationalities at the macro level, making what is estimated to be over thousands of discrete cultural groups, which are further divided into thousands of clan leaders. Each TCFS is identified with territorial integrity restricted by perceived and protected rights that are statutorily and mutually recognised as a *wut* in Dinka and led by an executive chief. In South Sudan, for millennia, traditional coping mechanisms and social cohesions around TCFSs headed by TALs have created a sense of nationhood identity. TCFSs created a sense of a self-styled traditional or societal nation-state system of governance. Under TCFSs, there is a public administrative system founded on a social contract dictated by mutuality, kinship, good neighbourliness and interdependence. Each TCFS existed, and continues to exist, in the form of a prototype modern nation-state with mutually recognised territory, peoples, morals, and spiritual, judicial and administrative jurisdictions protected and customarily administered by a communal youth legion. TCFSs existed and continue to exist as societal nation-states whose main economic mainstay was and continues to be a productive economy (livelihood) and a collaborative economy. TCFS is founded on self-reliance established on communal land ownership and family labour. In the modern political nation-state of the Republic of South Sudan, it could logically be proclaimed that TALs and TCFSs are explicitly recognised under the constitutional provisions and mandates of articles 166(6), 167, 168, 169(3) of SSTC 2011 and the entire LGA 2009.

CHAPTER TWO:
REVIEW OF RELATED LITERATURE

Introductory remarks

It is believed that vulnerability as a result of designed and enforced oppressive rules and exploitation by colonial masters and exclusion of vast populations in rural areas by successive 'national' governments in Khartoum, 1955 to 2004, are amongst the major causes of unrest in Old Sudan from 1956 (Malok 2009: 3). In the then Southern Sudan, now a sovereign Republic since 9 July 2011, two wars (1955–1972 and 1983–2004) were fought against such exploitation and marginalisation (Wassara 2007, Kuol 2008 and Malok 2009).

During the 1983–2004 war, TALs played pivotal roles in mobilising human and material wealth from local communities to win the liberation struggle (Kuol 2008: 69–83). TALs were also, and may continue now to be, instrumental in public administration, in mobilisation of rural peoples to build roads and schools, and in supporting education systems and administration of justice (Yom 2008, Wassara 2007, Malok 2009, and Arop 2011). However, in 2003 a policy of *Taking Towns to Rural Peoples* was envisioned (SPLM 2003). Since the implementation of the CPA in 2005 to the present day, this envisioned policy has been observed to attract huge political will and raise expectations amongst the rural population. The challenge is that the policy was not implemented as anticipated to be a tangible dividend of peace or in keeping with the policy directives made by leadership. Could potential success in realisation of the purpose of this goal be contingent on the level of recognition and involvement of TALs? If so, then what are the empirical facts, and what reconstructive policy, institutional framework and organisation culture are to be designed?

This literature review discusses and reflects on the concept of the envisioned policy of *Taking Towns to Rural Peoples*, examines the legacy of TALs and the validity of claims that TAL systems are irrelevant in the modern political nation-state of South Sudan. However, any discussion about livelihood and administering people in South Sudan is void of substance if it does not touch on land. Thus, this literature review includes issues of land ownership, rights, and dispossession of indigenous peoples in the name of 'public interest' and 'development'. It also examines the legal status of TAL systems in South Sudan and the significance of its roles. This section reviews the transformational leadership and change characteristics of TAL, as well as examining the roles of TALs in conflict management in South Sudan.

Concept of the policy *Taking Towns to Rural Peoples* in South Sudan

The concept was originally dubbed *Taking Towns to Rural Areas* (The SPLM Strategic Framework for War-to-Peace Program 2003). It was envisioned by Dr John Garang to improve the quality of life amongst the peoples living in rural areas as part of the national peace dividend. Dr Garang was inspired then by the renowned villagisation vision of Mwalimu Nyerere of Tanzania (Deng 2013:47). The underlying viewpoint of *Taking*

Towns to Rural Peoples is that globalisation should mean the coexistence of the global village with the effective and relevant traditional village.

The colonial British public administration in Africa opted for policies of indirect rule. They incorporated the administrative constituent units and governance positions of TCFSs and TALs. Framers of the vision of *Taking Towns to Rural Peoples* are assumed to have opted for a qualitative transformational change of the colonial perception of direct rule into direct governance, wider ownership and interactive participation of TCFSs and TALs in governance. This is perceived to ensure mutual recognition, unity in diversity. It is envisioned that modern institutions be taken to rural peoples for them to widely own them and to interactively engage with village, local government, and administrative state and national institutions of the executive and the legislature. *Taking Towns to Rural Peoples in South Sudan* envisions that TCFSs and TALs will be able to be collaboratively involved in identifying and implementing their own priorities. It is this suggested interweaving that is referred to as the twining between the modern political nation-state on the one hand and the TCFSs and TALs throughout the country on the other.

There are five arguments against the original designation of *Taking Towns to Rural Areas.* Firstly, it is null and void to talk of 'areas' to be developed without an institutionalised, inclusive process involving interactive participation, dedication of resources, and wider ownership by peoples in rural areas. Secondly, talking about areas and not the people suggests provision of basic social services as a gift considered by providers as top-down, external support assuming the 'uneducated' rural peoples could not perceive or be able to comprehend developmental issues. Thirdly, the naming indicates that elites have slipped into the footsteps of their colonial masters who excluded the roles of peoples in rural areas in governance decisions. Fourthly, it means the administrative structures, knowledge, attitudes and practices amongst elites of the decolonised nation-state persist in legitimising the control and exclusion of the rural population in decision-making. Fifth, *Taking Towns to Rural Peoples* should be comprehended as a strategy foreseen as a process that factors in elements of representative and selected/elected democratic entities engaging in mutuality and dialogue to consensually decide on matters affecting rural peoples.

Historical evolution of TAL institutions in South Sudan

Igga (2010: 31–46) elaborated that the Kush Kingdom was one of the greatest civilisations of the pre-historic world. Igga contends that:

> ... [b]ecause of wars of invasion for slaves and gold, foreigners destroyed this civilization. Such a civilization was built through the influence of warriors and kings, the traditional authority leaders. Colonizers later recognized the roles of these kings and warriors as traditional authority leaders purported by the self-exultation of invading colonizing kings who would not recognize local rulers as kings. ... In 710 BC Pianki at the age of twenty-one ruled Napata, which was one of the ancient

34

kingdoms in Sudan. Pianki decided to mobilize over 100,000 men and ordered the recapture of land... (Igga 2010:32)

Pianki is referred to as Pienk – meaning 'renowned' in Dinka (Deng 2013: 93–94). This suggests that TAL systems, structures and roles existed in ancient Sudan long before the advent of colonisers. The claim that TAL institutions were established by the British colonisers is historically inaccurate. Instead, the British colonisers fought to control and exclude, but later recognised, the TAL institutions while continuing to delegitimise and demonise the TCFSs.

An examination of the traditional socio-polity and administrative institutions in South Sudan suggests that the structures of *boma* administration as a level closer to the rural are relevant in South Sudan. This supposition is based on *boma* being founded on a traditional customary communal home for each of the 72 nationalities, which are estimated to be composed of thousands of discrete cultural entities. Each TCFS has a discrete pattern of diverse livelihoods, practices and norms and diverse cultural values that should be recognised and involved in any process of collaborative decision-making.

To reiterate, the TAL system in South Sudan is practised in separate patterns by each nationality or subnationality located in a traditional customary communal homeland. Each homeland is ascribed and identifies with territorial integrity restricted by perceived and protected rights that include rights to build dwellings, conduct burials, create shrines for worship, and compose sentimental and emphatic songs of belongingness, praise to homeland, self-exultation and efficacy. Such rights include privileges to cultivation, fishing, grazing of livestock, hunting, exploiting and managing forest products and hosting members of other communities for mutual coexistence. Consequently and for centuries these cohesive customary communal systems of governance have created the sense of identity of a self-styled nation-state with a communal collective army of age groups. Such rights and values inevitably rekindled and continued to create the bonds and fabrics of the sociopolitical, economic and cultural identity of a cohesive customary commune that is positively identical with and discrete from its neighbours, where each customary commune's societal desires accommodate individual desires to freely choose not to contravene the South Sudanese general will, as demonstrated in the historic 2011 referendum results. Similarly such general will was earlier demonstrated in historic collaborative resistance to slavery up to 1955 and beyond. The same general will ignited the zeal for liberty, peace and prosperity for all, irrespective of gender, faith, nationality and social strata.

Therefore it could be concluded that such customary communal federal administrations existed similar in form to a modern nation-state, but only lacked the modern perception of sovereignty recognised internationally and had no diplomatic connectivity and international treaties similar to modern present nation-states influenced by globalisation and information technology. However, since ancient times, under traditionally enthroned authorities, each nationality and customary communal federal system of administration in

South Sudan has opted for its form of customary communal federalism characterised by autonomous traditional governance and mutual coexistence within itself and with neighbouring communities.

Despite such patterns of customary communal federal systems, South–South collaborative resistance evolved from 658–664 AD with the invasion of the modern nation-state by Amr ibn al-'Aas. The essence of a fascist Arab nation-state marked this period in Old Sudan. Other colonisers, the Turks, followed in 1821, and this period was then followed by the 1883 Berlin Conference, which divided African territories according to colonial interests, giving them the rights to enslave and annex African land, enslave its citizens and to destroy its societies. Old Sudan came under British colonial rule from 1885 to 1955.

As a result, it could rightfully be claimed that the common identity of South Sudan was and shall continue to be moulded by a history of collaborative struggle and empathy for freedom and liberty. This could be due to a mutuality and interdependency based on unity in diversity. To enhance such a process there is a dire need to transform South Sudan into a society of commonality where every single culture counts, is recognised, is involved and is accountable to the South Sudanese general will for unity in diversity. It would be futile and frustrating to consider oppressive, exclusive, divisive and discriminating policies of assimilation that tend to create monoculturalism in a multicultural and multinational South Sudan that should embrace unity in diversity. South Sudanese diversity founded on mutual coexistence is attainable. Such TCFSs should be the foundation stone of our modern institutions.

In South Sudan, establishment of socioeconomic and traditional political groups and collective defence of settlements was largely dependent on prominent clan elders and spiritual and war leaders (Malok 2009: 5). This became clear with the advent of the Turks' invasion of the Sudan in 1821. After the collapse of the Ottoman Empire, the British and Egyptian colonialisation of Old Sudan followed. However, those conquests were resisted in South Sudan through the communities' traditional leadership. For instance, the Azande led their resistance through King Gbudwe. Names like Kon Anok, Dhieu Alam, Biar Abit and Ariath Kon, amongst others, in the Dinka nationalities and Guek Ngundeng of Nuer led their communities in such resistance (Malok 2009: 5). Besides that, Arop (2012: 26–53) concluded that in those decades of wars against external invaders, TALs waged resistance and liberation wars. It is claimed that because of such roles fulfilled by TAL, South Sudan never came to a proper and well-organised system of governance, until it achieved independence in 2011 (Deng 2013: 47).

In separate writings, Arop (2012: 1–17), Malok (2009: 4–26) and Yom (2005: 35–51) concur in their explanation that the period of 1821–1955 was characterised by invasions, annexation of land, enslavement, wanton killings and looting and destruction of resources. Wars of liberation occurred in the period of 1955–1972 and later in 1983–2005. Kuol's (2008: 69–83) findings on the roles of TAL provided evidence that TAL played a transformational leadership role in mobilising local material and human resources that helped the liberation efforts in the period 1983–2004. Wassara (2007: 7) emphasises the democratic nature of TAL: 'Traditional Authority Leadership has been heritably selected and appointed but also practices have shown that open nomination and democratic elections have been witnessed recently'. In modern South Sudan, the Government of South Sudan according to the Local Government Act (LGA) 2009, section 115 recognises two types of TAL, which are the kingdoms amongst the Anyuak People of Jonglei State and Cholo Peoples of Upper Nile State and others with mixed systems of authority. The Kingdom of Azande People is yet to be officially recognised by the government as perceived and valued by the Azande People. TCFSs are a sound foundation for any peoples-centred modern institutions, as a form of inclusive and good governance closer to the peoples.

Significance of the role of TAL institutions in South Sudan

According to Wassara (2007:8), traditionally, preservation of culture and adherence to common laws, values and informal economic transaction and resolving disputes amongst the rural peoples are important roles of TALs in South Sudan. In addition, TAL institutions have a special position considered to arbitrate restoration of harmony and adjudicate in disputes using traditionally based restorative justice. Their communities perceive TALs as guardians and spiritual protectors of culture, social norms and values. Their institutions serve as a foundation to seek blessing for the cleansing and wellbeing of their communities. For a community's members, to ensure that values, principles and practices of mutual interdependence through kinship and economic promoting mechanisms are protected, preserved and adhered to, would choose as a value to trust the TALs and their institutions. Therefore the TAL systems promote and preserve national and local social and political capital (Deng 2013: 192) in South Sudan.

My personal experience supports perceptions that TAL institutional roles enhance traditional coping mechanisms amongst rural peoples throughout the country. For example the Twic community from Warrap State, which is my homeland, may illustrate this situation. The Twic community, before current expansions, was known as Twic Bol Nyuol, then Twic Bol Chol, whose community foci (court and community forum) were popularly known as Tiitchok Bol Chol, literally meaning 'under the mahogany tree of Bol Chol'. It later became Kurnyok-chok during the reign of Nyuol Bol (Nyuol Managar) and is now popularly known as the Kebo-chok of Executive Chief Garang Nyuol. Similarly, in the Pannyok *payam* of Twic county there is Lach-chok at Aerich and subsequently Rualmakam, literally meaning the Ruaal of Chief Court, at the village of Wunlit Goi Awakmacham. The function of such community foci is to conduct public forums, to routinely consult on their livelihood, and to adjudicate through a traditionally founded restorative justice system in their customary courts. The venues are used for public rallies and hosting guests visiting the community. Similar experiences were observed during the study tour in South Africa, Ghana and Botswana. Governments, visitors and communities used Kgotla for the same purposes. In one Kgotla visited, there was evidence of a totem of the community and written history indicating the essence and pride of the communities.

In the photo below is a chronicle engraved in stone of a totem and written history of the Boora Tshidi Community, symbolised by a history of their founding father, Besele I, who commanded a tribal regiment against an invading British Army from 1899 to 1900.

Figure 1: Inscription of Kgosi Besele I, Commander-in-Chief of Matsetse Regiment in 1899

Seen below is Kgosi (Executive Chief) Engineer Jeff Kgotleng Montshioa, in his family's 200-year-old Kgotla of Baralong Boora Tshidi community, welcoming and briefing South Sudanese delegates at Kgotla on the roles of TALs in the community.

41

Figure 2: Kgosi Engineer Jeff K. Montshioa, who holds an advanced degree in engineering, briefing the delegation at Kgotla of Baralong Boora Tshidi at the Barolong District Traditional Council, Mafikeng, North West Province, South Africa, 17 January 2013

Two opinion polls conducted by the International Republican Institute (IRI) in 2011 and 2013 in South Sudan (Appendices 6 and 7) collected views that asked respondents to choose whom they thought very favourable, favourable, unfavourable or very unfavourable. The respondents answered: traditional leader 39% very favourable, 39% favourable, 13% unfavourable and 5% very unfavourable. This is compared to their response concerning the president, with 50% very favourable, 32% favourable, 10% unfavourable and 4% very unfavourable, and the state governor, with 24% very favourable, 32% favourable,

18% unfavourable and 20% very unfavourable (see Appendix 6). However, a rise in favour of TALs was detected in a similar survey repeated in 2013. The respondents rated TALs the highest, with 59% very favourable, 28% favourable, 7% unfavourable and 3% unfavourable. This is compared with the county commissioner, with 32% very favourable, 40% favourable, 14% unfavourable and 8% very unfavourable (see Appendix 7).

Governor Jemma Nunu Kumba, the first South Sudanese female governor appointed in Western Equatoria state (2007–2010), stated in 2008 (www.gurtong.net) that:

...the chiefs are important because they live with the people. They know the problems of the people. Their people listen to them; so when they talk to the people they listen. We, the government are a bit far from the people, but the chiefs are living right there with their people. Traditionally, every citizen lives under the authority of those traditional leaders and chiefs. They know how to mobilise, they know how to pass messages and their people respect them. So my administration will see that this relationship is sustained. I am now glad that they have been able to form a council, which is a forum where they can come and raise common issues facing them and lay common strategies. It is also a channel through which the government can reach them with services...

Patrice Waga of Eastern Equatoria state (Semonse and Kurimoto 2008: 116) stated that:

...At times the government's presence in the countryside is poorly felt. This has let residents to seek ways of filling the gap and Monyomiji [youth] are at the forefront of seeking alternatives. They are involved in every crucial decision-making meeting in the community and are charged with ensuring the implementation of decisions reached...

Chief Mogga Otto Lomeri, Chief of Ngulere *boma*, Liria Payam, Juba County, referred to their collaborative efforts that resulted in a primary school and health centres being built in their *boma*. Chief Moga expressed his delight that in his *boma*, community members were encouraged to take part in training courses and workshops on peacebuilding, as well as on horticulture, beekeeping, poultry breeding and adoption of improved stoves.

The significance of TAL institutions could be employed to promote collaborative dialogue and learning in South Sudan. This significance is largely visible in customary forums like the chief's tree used for community meetings and consultation in rural South Sudan. The Kgotla in Botswana and South Africa and the chiefs' palace in Ghana demonstrate sufficient evidence that the envisioned process of *Taking Towns to Rural Peoples* could be sustainably attained and widely owned through recognition, incorporation and involvement of TAL institutions in South Sudan.

Also, to demonstrate the relevance of TALs, in Northern Bahr el Ghazal State, the president of the traditional court in Warawar Peace Market, Chief Deng Luol Akuei of Abiem Community in Eastern Aweil County, initiated collaboration with a community leader of Misseriya Arab, the late Ahmed Hammed, and his successor, Adam Mohammed Ahmed of Southern Kordofan. In 1991, these two TALs of arch-conflicting Dinka and Misseriya communities invented a corridor of peace mechanism and a peace market popularly known as Warawar Peace Market. This social contract and political capital was envisioned, institutionalised and collaboratively implemented with huge success amidst armed conflict that resulted in several attacks on the corridor and the market itself. Mechanisms of conflict mitigation, mediation and negotiated access were institutionalised as was envisioned, reframed and negotiated by the TALs of the two communities during the then Sudan war (1983–2004). Today, despite the strained cross-border relationship between Sudan north and South Sudan, Warrap Peace Market is flourishing. Because of such conflict mitigation and being mutuality envisioned, established and supervised by TALs of the Dinka and Misseriya communities, Warawar Peace Market could not be affected by border closure.

Legal status of TAL institutions in South Sudan

SSTC 2011 article 166(6)(c) mandates local government to '...encourage the involvement of communities and community-based organisations on matters of local government, promote dialogue among them on matters of local interest.' Article 166(6)(i) mandates all levels of government in the Republic of South Sudan to '... acknowledge and incorporate the role of Traditional Authority and customary law in the local government system.' Article 166(6)(j) mandates to '...involve communities in decision related to the exploration of natural resources in their areas and promote a safe healthy environment.' SSTC 2011 article 167(1) mandates that' 'The institutions, status and role of Traditional Authority, according to customary law, are recognised under this constitution.' Also article 168(1) sets terms of office such that: 'Legislation of the states shall provide for the roles of Traditional Authority as an institution at the local government level on matters affecting local communities...'. A similar mandate under article 168(2) states that: 'Legislation at the national and state levels shall provide for the establishment, composition, functions and duties of Councils of Traditional Authority Leaders (COTALs).' Article 169(3) demands that national government should promote and encourage the participation of the people in the formulation of its development policies and programs. This could be attained through a national COTAL.

Article 169(7) also mandates respect for each level of government in discharging their duties and that quality of life and dignity of peoples are promoted without discrimination or exclusion on grounds of gender, religion, political affiliation, ethnicity, nationality, language or locality. Article 2 of SSTC 2011 states: 'Sovereignty is vested in the people and shall be exercised by the State through its democratic and representative institutions established by this

Constitution.' This should be read together with article 167(1) of SSTC 2011. Article 35(1) of SSTC 2011 mandates that all levels of government and their organs, institutions and citizens shall be guided by the principles contained in the constitution.

COTALs' roles in cementing *unity in diversity* in South Sudan

Provisions of article 168(2) and article 168(1) of SSTC 2011 mandate the legislation of roles, status, establishment, composition, functions and duties of COTALs at national and state levels respectively. Central Equatoria state, Eastern Equatoria state, Western Equatoria state, Upper Nile state and Jonglei state have fulfilled the mandates of article 168(1) by enacting the State COTAL Act 2011 (see Appendix 8). However, none of those states has translated a State COTAL Act into the envisaged institutionalised systems as mandated by the COTAL Act. Also it is observed that provisions on the composition of COTALs in each of the states and the number of delegates to a national COTAL are not responsive to the constitutional provisions and realities of cultural diversity in each state. There are legal gaps that do not fulfil the constitutional mandate that the state COTAL should be inclusive of all nationalities and their cultures. Likewise, the national COTAL should be inclusive of all 72 nationalities – the peoples of South Sudan. Decisions in COTAL forums should be by consensus and allow collaborative learning and networking so that there should be no nationalities left out at any phase because of population size. It is anticipated that COTALs at state and in national consultative routinised forums shall be inclusive of all nationalities.

Potential role of TAL institutions as factors of good governance

In line with the idea of empowering local grassroots roles to participate in governance process, according to Gaventa and Camilo (1999: 2), citizens' participation in the governance process takes three dimensions. The first is social and project participation. According to them, social participation means allowing the public to take ownership of development projects with wider ownership and interactive participation. Participation in development projects and programs by the community, according to Gaventa and Camilo, becomes a tool for or means of strengthening their relevance, quality, ownership and sustainability. The second dimension is political participation. Political participation, according to Nie and Verba (1972: 2) as quoted in Gaventa and Camilo (1999: 3), is defined as 'those legal activities by private citizens that are more or less directly aimed at influencing the section of governmental personnel and/or the action they take'. For them, it means taking in the process of formulation, passage and implementation of public policies. The main concern is inaction by citizens aimed at influencing decisions taken by public representatives and officials. Similarly, Richardson (1983) and Cunill (1991) in Gaventa and Camilo (1999: 4) consider political participation more as a process which is associated with representative democracy and indirect participation of the citizens in governing the process. Wider political participation of the citizens in the governing process is, in my view, very crucial for emerging countries like South Sudan because it can help citizens through their representatives at county, state and national levels to hold public officials accountable for their actions. This is in line with my view that traditional leadership authority should be given wider participative roles in the policymaking process and its implementation at all levels as mandated by article 168 of SSTC 2011.

The third dimension is the participatory method. According to Gaventa and Camilo (1999), participatory methods are found in the field of political participation and include the vectors of education, enhancing the awareness of rights and responsibilities of the citizens, lobbying and advocacy, often aimed at developing a more informed citizenry who could hold elected representative more accountable for their political actions. These methods are meant to empower grassroots communities in order to ensure participation in the governance process of the country. Other examples of the comparative analysis of traditional governance systems in different countries include Royal Bafokeng Holding in South Africa[1], a community-based business run and managed by a traditional authority, and Grameen Bank in Bangladesh[2], with its use of non-bankable assets and mores of trust and social capital as collateral for the local community to access financing benefits in order to promote their local businesses. All of these are traditional governance systems meant to develop the local communities through their traditional leaders. In

---

[1] See www.bafokengholdings.org.
[2] See www.grameen.org.

this regard, my argument is that such local governance systems can also be applied to empower the grassroots communities through their traditional system in South Sudan. It can also be argued that South Sudan, being a multicultural society with different nationalities, needs governance systems that empower the local grassroots communities, which should be realised by empowering the TALs to be involved in the governance and social and economic development of the country.

Mistaken view of the irrelevance of TAL in South Sudan

The incident of the burning of T-shirts bearing the emblem of the House of Nationalities (HoN), which was denounced by Dr Garang in New Site in 2003, sent the wrong signals. This single incident was situational, and Dr Garang's criticism of it was intended to stem out the suspected influence by then Morgue Group. This group of South Sudanese intellectuals mistakenly openly ridiculed the vision of New Sudan (Deng 2013: 31). The group instead proposed their alternative vision reframed as a replacement to Dr Garang's envisioned New Sudan of inclusivity, justice, peace and prosperity for all, irrespective of gender, faith and nationality. A published pamphlet, christened as the HoN, gave messages that were either misunderstood, misrepresented or mis-deciphered. There is evidence that before and after that incident of the T-shirt burning the SPLM program continued to give favourable regard to TAL institutions in the administration of liberated areas and in mobilising war efforts (Kuol 2008). A similar occurrence happened with the famous South–South political dialogue that was once objected to, but the process was later allowed under the auspices of Dr Garang. In 2005, following the signing of the CPA, Dr Garang presided over a South–South dialogue, then hosted by the Moi Foundation. President Kiir rekindled the process later, making him an icon of peace and reconciliation.

The spread of small arms and the subsequent insecurity arising in rural areas is giving a misleading reading to foreign researchers that the TAL system is weakened. This misreading appears to emanate from three factors. Firstly, it may be the result of a misleading translation by South Sudanese elites whose perception could not make sense of the structures of TAL because of prejudice against the TAL. This is further blamed on the essence of education and acquired attitudes inculcated through training and practices purported by their colonial masters. Those colonial masters engaged in extraction and exploitation with policies designed to undermine the colonised peoples and their TAL system, not to rejuvenate their efficacy and ability to rule or to decide for themselves (Hoehne 2008: 5-14). The kernel, origin and hierarchy of paramount chiefs, executive chiefs, subchiefs, headmen and elders, besides some religious authority, are not artificial, as misleadingly proclaimed by Hoehne (2008: 19), who stated that the colonisers created TAL institutions. Hoehne contradicted himself in his quote (Hoehne 2008: 14) to Johnson 1986: 63–76) who found that:

> ... in the late 19th century, first the Turco-Egyptian and then Anglo-Egyptian administrations set out to establish control over southern Sudanese territories... initially the

British tried to simply take over and co-opt traditional authorities and customary law... Soon, however, they realised that effective administration was impossible in this way... when they used force to extract tributes and control, the colonisers faced rebellion from side of Nuer...

Hoehne's views that chiefs were artificially created by colonisers and that TAL systems are not relevant to modernised South Sudan should be dismissed. Yom (2005: 35–51) concurs in his work on the Nuer rebellion, citing it as revolt against corrupt Greek traders who, with the British administrators, adopted the practice of looting through underpricing livestock sold by Nuers and collecting ridiculous unarranged taxes without return in services. The British Administrator was engaged in antisocial behaviour. He was abducting Nuer girls and abusing them. Both the traders and the administrators were ambushed and killed, as was approved and demanded by the communities and their leaders. Attempts to arrest the killers were resisted, because the decision to kill the two foreigners was sanctioned by elders, warriors, the chiefs, the spiritual leaders and their followers.

Hoehne (2008: 14) acknowledges the cruel human rights abuse and humiliation of TALs by invaders. In that, Hoehne quoted Leonardi (2007: 544) that colonisers used coercive or punitive measure to seize and beat local leaders to give in to colonial masters' directives. This confession of use of coercive measures indicates that TAL systems were in existence and were putting up resistance against capitulation and attempting to undermine the authority of the colonial nation-state. While Hoehne's work seems to support similar traditional institutions in north Sudan, Hoehne explicitly scoffed at the non-feudalistic systems in then Southern Sudan by using the word 'so-called' to refer to the liberal and traditional democracies of the egalitarian societies of Nuer and Dinka, amongst others, which had actually existed since inception and were not created by colonisers as falsely claimed by some circles. Tier and Dhal's (2005: 66) reference to the Native Courts Ordinance 1932 might have suggested to other researchers that the process signalled the start of the existence of TALs. But Tier and Dhal (2005: 33) made it clear that when the Anglo-Egyptian Condominium was established in 1899, a unique situation thus arose when traditional structures existed side by side with those of the modern nation-state. Colonisers renamed and exploited already existing leadership systems in the colonised societies, but did not 'invent' TAL structures themselves. This explains why TALs are respected, because their existence is inherited in traditional socio-polity and cultural systems. Separate works by Wassara (2007), Yom (2008), Kuol (2008), Arop (2012), Malok (2009) and Deng (2013) provide empirical evidence of the importance of TAL systems in South Sudan. They wrote on how TAL institutions have been instrumental in mobilising their communities to resist external invasions and encourage their followers to engage in development, public administration and administration of customary justice. As also observed, Deng (2013: 9) explained that prejudices concealed the historical facts of the Kush Kingdom of ancient Sudan, which was larger than the then disintegrated New Kingdom of Egypt, and its dominance extended over the present geographical area of Egypt. Quoting Dr Timothy Kendal and Dan Morrison (National Geographic News: 18 June 2007), the Kush Kingdom borders and influence reached the ancient Holy Land of the birth of Christ (Deng 2013). Hoehne and others might have followed the fashion of unfairly presenting the history of TALs. In attempts to seek collaboration and support from one development agent and in a separate encounter with some South Sudanese elites, my research was once criticised for focusing on what is already regarded by 'experts' as archaic and irrelevant in modern South Sudan. This dangerous trend should be corrected to ensure that local capacities are tapped.

Transformational leadership characteristics of TALs in South Sudan

In Dinka Language (language of the author) a leader is *abiok ruel,* apparently meaning a guide to a herd. Like a herd of buffalos or elephants, in this context it implies a purposeful community with a vision being guided by a leader. Roger Gill (2008: 96) states: 'a clear vision without effective, emotional, spiritual and behavioural leadership is impotent'. To be effective a transformational leader is that person who 'ensures that the vision is translated into reality'. Lecture notes by Professor Badeg (2012) indicate that researchers have agreed that there are as many different definitions of leadership as diverse as those who contributed to defining leadership.

In expounding upon similar views, Roger Gill (2008: 36) states that there are various types of leadership theories, two of which in my view are particularly relevant to the roles of TALs in South Sudan. The first are trait leadership theories, also known as 'great man' theories, which postulate common qualities or characteristics of effective leaders. This theory raises the question on whether such qualities are inherited or acquired. In accordance with beliefs and customs that make up social and political capital and the TAL institutional culture in rural South Sudan, their communities select TALs from and amongst royal families. In doing so, they value the historical legacy of individual leaders who led their peoples during difficult times and whose ancestors have a record of meting justice amongst their peoples. The assumption is that descendants of historical leaders may emulate their forefathers, as they are influenced through induction and family culture. The second type are theories of transformational leadership, defined as 'new leadership', which comprises visionary, charismatic and transformational leadership qualities. 'Transformational leadership occurs when leaders raise people's motivation to act and to create a sense of higher purpose' (Gill 2008: 36).

As mentioned above, it is also true that it was the TALs and their institutions that played a transformational and change leadership role in mobilising human and material resources to support the efforts of the war of liberation by providing services to soldiers at the frontline (Kuol 2008: 69–83). Kuol's work demonstrates the great and effective transformational and change leadership characteristics of the TALs. As mentioned earlier, in the 1920s during the

British colonial administration in Sudan, TALs were recognised as mediators or connectors between the local communities and the British colonial administrators (Yom 2007, Malok 2009 and Arop 2012). Bass and Riggio's (2006: 5) work is paraphrased here to describe TAL roles as transformational leadership in their functions because they motivated their subjects in rural South Sudan to protect their lives, land and properties, which were targets of invading foreigners. Convincingly, the Whole-person Leadership Model adopted by Covey (2004:122) states that leadership is a process of '...communicating people's worth and potentials so clearly that they come to see it in themselves'. Likewise, Lee and King (2001: 9–10) consider that, to be an effective transformational and change leader, a leader is idealised by followers because such a person uses certain significant leadership characteristics to guide and coordinate followers' efforts through all process of '...changing contexts and demands, vision, values, self-awareness and balance'. Considering such historical evidence, it is false to claim that TAL systems have now lost relevance. Again, it is not true that the colonisers created the TAL system in South Sudan. Colonial masters incorporated TAL systems to connect the colonisers with the colonised rural majority. The colonisers did not create TAL systems as claimed. The research conducted here suggests it would prove healthier to now engage in recognising and connecting with the status and involvement of TAL institutions in moulding the modern South Sudan.

TALs' transformational leadership in conflict mediation in South Sudan

During war time in South Sudan, TALs played significant and pivotal roles as public administrators in the provision of social services, maintenance of law and order, and administration of justice amongst rural communities (Kuol 2008: 69–83 and Wassara 2007). TAL institutions granted the necessary backup support in the process of peace dialogue within and amongst their communities. Also, during and throughout the CPA implementation, TALs played crucial roles in mobilising their communities to register and to effectively participate in the 2008 census, 2010 general elections and finally in the 2011 referendum in South Sudan (Deng 2013: 158). This is an indication that TALs are effective partners at all levels. Therefore, it is evident that TALs, through their individual existence and collective roles through COTALs, could serve as a sensible conduit between their communities and the government at national, state and local government levels to enhance the process of realisation of *Taking Towns to Rural Peoples* in South Sudan.

Suspected flaws in land ownership and land tenure in South Sudan

The modern political nation-state evolved from feudalism of oppressive perception that royal and ruling families administered and used to subjugate people and land through appointed landlords. Within this system landlords were selected and appointed subject to their knighthood and ability to fight or to organise armies and slaves to defend the feudal state. Landlords remitted, as taxes, farm produce, booties of war and slaves to the royal families. In turn royal families granted landlords and the warlords rights to allot land to smallholder farmers, the peasants, who paid landlords in form of farm produce as a price for access to land and protection by the warlords. Smallholders engaged slaves and fed them to work with no pay.

In contrast to the oppressive, exploitative and exclusive colonial state, Johari (2010: 47) suggested that:

> ...there are four elements that constitute a people-centred modern nation-state. Firstly, the people – population – that live in peace, security and liberty. Secondly is the land and territorial integrity that is enabling productivity to meet the basic needs and production. Thirdly, the government that is able to protect the life and the property including protecting territorial integrity against any aggression. Fourthly, the sovereignty and supreme power and authority that is unchallenged in safeguarding the internal and external socio-political economic and cultural sphere of the citizens...[sic]

As mentioned above in this report, the essence of colonising indigenous peoples in Africa included efforts to dispossess land from its owners and their TALs. This could be said to be the origin of the word Crown Land now by extension state land. Colonisers legislated land not for communities but for the invading new masters of the colonising nation-state in Africa, Australia, North Africa and both North and South America, Canada and indeed in Old Sudan. Professor Okoth's work in 2003, concluded that:

> .... The perception of 'land belongs' to government in Southern Sudan arose from a series of pre-emptive measures enacted by the British and the Arab/Muslim government out of Khartoum. The two colonizers purported a view that land in Southern Sudan was, by reason of lack of private registration, is vested in the national government in Khartoum. These measures against local perception of communal land ownership were mandated through four legal documents. First, was the Land Settlement and Registration Act (LSRA) 1925. Second was the Land Acquisition Act (LAA) 1930. Third was the Unregistered Land Act (ULA) 1970... The most recent was the Civil Transactions Act (CTA) 1984...

The LSRA 1925 was enacted to facilitate the adjudication of land and its registration as private property throughout the colony. That process assumed, however, that documentation establishing such private ownership rights or compelling evidence to that effect could be produced. The LAA 1930 gave the state, the 'national government', the power to compulsorily acquire private property for 'public purposes' upon payment of compensation. Although the 'public purposes' requirement was not defined, it is clear that the legislation was intended also to facilitate the acquisition of land for private investment by close associates in power. This trend can be observed today in the Republic of South Sudan. Community lands in Juba, Torit, Wau,

Malakal and Yei, for example have suffered expropriation and land grabbing by well-placed individuals. Local orders are released without due consideration to constitutional mandates to involve TALs as mandated by article 166(6) of SSTC 2011.

The ULA 1970, which was enacted after independence, was a more insidious piece of legislation. It was a blanket attempt to appropriate not merely radical title to unregistered land but full ownership rights thereof by the state. The legislation, which was intended to apply to 'lands in all places in the Sudan whether or not in any such place the system of land registration is in place', proclaimed, inter alia, that: 'All land of any kind whether waste, forest, occupied or unoccupied, which is not registered before the commencement of this Act shall ... be the property of the government and shall be deemed to have been registered as such as if the provisions of the Land Settlement and Registration Act 1925 have been duly complied with'. The target clearly was to enable the oppressive government of Sudan to exert proprietary power over land (especially in the then Southern Sudan) that had for centuries been held under the system of customary land law, and administered by communities through their recognised governance structures. And although the CTA 1984 repeals both the LSRA 1925 and the ULA 1930, it saves all actions previously taken under them. Thus, shortly before conclusion of the CPA 2009, nearly all land in Southern Sudan was technically the property of the high-handed government in Khartoum.

In South Sudan, similar to all other former colonies in Africa, the essence of misperception of land assumed to be unconsciously belonging to government has its historical legacies rooted in the colonial mentality, which should be reviewed. Intellectuals, professionals and government officials, unfortunately, recite blindly the words that land belongs to government. These mentally oppressed individuals and groups should be liberated. Those governments with bad faith that ruled Southern Sudan before 9 July 2005 were influenced by perceptions alien to South Sudanese societies and their livelihoods linked to land ownership. The colonial nation-state aimed to exploit indigenous resources while excluding traditional authority systems in governance. It is no surprise that their first attempt was to disconnect indigenous communities, with impunity, from their land. The sovereignty of the Government of Republic of South Sudan is vested in its peoples' values, philosophy and laws. Land is explicitly and expressly with legal holding that land belongs to the communities as comes under SSTC 2011 article 171 (7): Rights in land owned by the Government of Southern Sudan shall be exercised through the appropriate or designated level of government in Southern Sudan, which shall recognise customary land rights under customary land laws. SSTC 2011 article 171(8) mandates all levels of government in Southern Sudan shall institute a process to progressively develop and amend the relevant laws to incorporate customary laws, practices, local heritage and international trends and practices. SSTC article 171(5) mandates that all lands traditionally and historically held by local communities or their members shall be defined, held, managed and protected by law in Southern Sudan. In SSTC 2011, no explanation is given for omitting the provisions of ICOSS article 180(5), which stated:

...Customary seasonal rights to land shall be protected, provided that these access rights shall be regulated by the respective states taking into account the need to protect agricultural production, community peace and harmony, and without unduly interfering with or degrading the primary ownership interest in the land, in accordance with customary law...

SSTC 2011 article 171(10) mandates that communities and persons enjoying rights in land shall be consulted and their views duly taken into account in decisions to develop subterranean natural resources in the area in which they have rights, and they shall share in the benefits of that development. To attain inclusive good governance in modern South Sudan, such legal provisions should be enforced to give rights to host communities to benefit from land revenues collected in expansion of urban centres. The proceeds could contribute to financing the achievement of *Taking Towns to Rural Peoples*.

At Naivasha Kenya, on 7 January 2004, the SPLM and National Congress Party (NCP) signed the Agreement on Wealth Sharing that later made up part of the CPA 2005. Section 2.2 of the agreement mandates that the parties record that the regulation of land tenure, usage and exercise of rights in land is to be a concurrent competency exercised at the appropriate levels of government. Section 2.3 agreed that '... Rights in land owned by the Government of Sudan shall be exercised through the appropriate or designated levels of government'. The issue of land was expressly addressed under section 2.4: The parties agreed that a process be instituted to progressively develop and amend the relevant laws to incorporate customary laws and practices, local heritage and international trends and practices. This is an explicit recognition that land belongs to communities. Evidence is provided by ICOSS article 180(5).

Ill-informed South Sudanese elites who are suspected of suffering from the curse of cluelessness and individualism demonstrated by professional administrators (Bolman and Deal 2003: 6–8), without a careful investigative mind, would today claim that Dr Garang's negotiated position on land in Naivasha was limited to protecting South Sudan land from Khartoum. But the truth is that the position of the SPLM was ideologically based on justice and a true liberty viewpoint to restore land to its rightful owners, the indigenous occupant communities and not to be 'owned' by government. This injustice was perceived to be correct in land grabbing in Europe, Australia, the Americas and some parts of Africa, where indigenous and rightful owners of land were not only indiscriminately webbed out, but survivors are disposed from land ownership as communities are now excluded from decision-making processes.

In reference to land rights, Tier and Dhal's (2005: 36) work mentioned that land rights is perceived: '...to assert certain groups' rights including building of dwellings, cultivation, fishing, grazing of livestock, hunting, exploiting and managing forest products. Such rights inevitably create a bond of social and political identity and cohesion...'. Constitutionally and in accordance with prevailing political will and customary practices in South Sudan, land rights have been recognised, and it is wrong to legislate against such backdrops because it contradicts the law of natural justice and SSCT 2011. The perception that extorting land from communities in the name of development while considering that land as not having economic value should entitle the community to own shares in any business hosted by the community and is influenced by injustice inculcated by colonial masters whose interest is to grab land in exclusion of ancestral land owners. It is a mistake that is blindly adopted by any peoples-centred national government by and for the peoples.

Tier and Dhal (2005: 56) explain another challenging phenomenon that determinates the coexistence and mutuality in South Sudan. This anomaly is in the crime and the civil wrongs mentality amongst Dinka and Nuer. It is relevant because it could be borrowed and expanded to explain many similar erroneous perceptions that dominate the thinking of the elites-turned-rulers with a tendency to exclude TALs and the rural majority. To paraphrase Tier and Dhal (2005: 56–65): stealthy and forcible detachment of cows and looting of cattle during fights are not regarded as a crime between Nuer and Dinka. This likely perception could be extended to explain the rampant child abduction in some other parts of South Sudan, where it is regarded as a source of regeneration and heroic possession to abduct children from other communities. Such perceptions are repugnant and should be eliminated through dialogue and law enforcement by ways and means involving TAL systems. The danger is that such erroneous perceptions have found their way into the essence of the 'modern' nation-state where a centralised system is created in the name of the executive, legislature and law enforcement in exclusion of TCFSs. Excluding TCFSs suggests that the elites in urban areas in South Sudan have replaced the colonisers and appointed themselves as new rulers distant from their community and who in addition have excluded the rural majority and their TALs in the decision-making process. The elites leading these 'modern' systems have allowed themselves to allocate (extort) income from natural resources and collected tax as their salaries and benefits. In his teachings about the need to promote self-reliance through supporting rural transformation President Kiir on 21 May 2010 advised that:

> ...We also have to wean ourselves away of the habit of depending on the bonanza of oil revenues. Nations cannot be built on windfall profits. Consequently, the portion of oil revenues that may be dedicated to rural transformation shall be devoted, in real terms, to that transformation...[Oil revenues] are to be utilized for uplifting the life of the rural populace and raising their capacity to better till the land, upgrading agriculture and animal husbandry practices, ensuring better marketing and distribution facilities for rural produce...

Another predicament considered to be fuelling corruption is that communities from whom suspected looters originate may regard grabbing and misappropriation of national wealth as cleverness and shrewdness. Though the law criminalises, it is regarded by some elements as unnecessary disruption of the right to eat and to manipulate the resources and jobs. The worst of these trends is that land extortion from the community is not regarded as a crime but a legitimate act mandated by unlawful policies. It is frightening that those decision-makers born in towns regard community land ownership within the value of a plot allocation in urban areas. They do not share a consciousness of the value of natural land that affects the livelihood of the rural peoples who own the land. The colonial mentality that land is worthless is a threat and makes indigenous inhabitants vulnerable. Such perceptions contradict the natural justices and are against the revolutionary ideals in South Sudan that aimed at freedom from exploitation and exclusion. Use of land for development should factor in the inhabitants' interest. In this process, land should be regarded as an asset with a value in capital as in any company hosted on land owned by a community with customary land right.

The foundation of South Sudan explicitly subscribed to a type of government, guiding principles, economic goals, political goals, levels of government, and devolution of powers in accordance with articles 2, 35, 36, 37, 47, 48 and 49 respectively. Articles 167 and 168 of SSTC 2011 and section 19(3) of LGA 2009 mandate terms of governance with regard to TAL systems. Article 166 of SSTC mandates communities and their leaders to be consulted and involved on issues that affect them most. In Dinka knowledge, attitude and practice, liberation struggle was dubbed "luel ee piny" meaning struggle and sacrifice for land to be repossessed from invaders. However, notwithstanding the victory, the freedom fighters-turned-rulers unfortunately followed in the footsteps of the colonisers by excluding TAL in decision-making, and with indignity adopted unjust perceptions and policies on land rights. It is my opinion that it is illegal for current generations to be predisposed of land because past generations and future ones are being robbed of what is identified as spiritual, economic, a part of identity and the mainstay of livelihood. It is wrong to subject South Sudanese to being landless and dispossessed of their community land rights. The remedy is to recognise TALs and to involve them in the proposed Land Board at all levels. Such recognition of the status and roles of TAL as enshrined in SSTC 2011 could enhance TAL transformational and change leadership characteristics to provide needed social and institutional factors in timely realisation of the goal of *Taking Towns to Rural Peoples* in rural South Sudan.

CHAPTER THREE:
DESIGN OF THE STUDY AND
RESEARCH METHODOLOGY

Design of the study

This research employed three approaches. The first approach was a desk study, which reviewed available primary and secondary literature. The following themes and topics were investigated: (a) the supposition that involving TAL systems and structure could be a successful social conduit for transforming the policy *Taking Towns to Rural Peoples* into an institutionalised framework, an organisational culture and practice in rural South Sudan, and a bridge to a budding newly found nation-state; (b) the historical legacy and roles of TAL institutions amongst the rural peoples that could enhance interactive participation in policymaking and policy implementation; (c) the level of cluelessness and presumed level of adherence to explicit policies in SSTC 2011 and LGA 2009 which mandated recognition of status and roles of TAL and mandated their involvement in the composition, structures and functions of national, state and local government; (d) the level of awareness and appraisal of whether the constitutional mandates were being fulfilled at national, state, and local government levels in an attempt to identify challenges and to suggest solutions; and (e) the possible legal gaps suspected to be the cause of inadequate adherence to the constitutional mandate as noted during dialogue with respondents, the focus group, on possible legal and institutional reframing to incorporate TAL roles in the composition, structures and functions of the executive, the legislature and judicial branches at all levels.

Secondly, the study explored field expositions and acquaintances, and utilised briefings from the host communities and governmental officials in Botswana, South Africa and Ghana. Observations were made and documented during the familiarisation and study tour. The purpose of the tour was to learn about the status, composition and functions of TALs in accordance with their constitutions, statutes and judicial decisions, and political debates surrounding the TALs in government and rural areas in the countries visited. Members of the tour included TALs and representatives of the executive and legislative branches of the Government of South Sudan. This initiative exposed a number of traditional leaders and representatives of the government in the Republic of South Sudan to the ideas and practices of how service delivery, public administration and administration of justice are sectors where responsibility rests with the TALs and their communities in rural areas and some aspects of livelihood in urban areas. Participants in the tour were also informed about the exotic model of bicameral legislatures in Botswana and routinised consultative forums in South Africa and Ghana. Also participants listened to and dialogued on perceptions that TAL systems are elected/selected to a separate local, provincial and national House of Chiefs with the purpose of routinised consultative procedures but with no legislative powers except for advice and consultation on matters referred to the House of Chiefs by the respective legislature and/or executive. However, participants learnt how such national, provincial and district houses are mandated by the constitution to be routinely consulted by respective levels of government on matters affecting traditions and livelihood in rural Ghana, Botswana and South Africa.

Thirdly, an opinion survey was conducted using a closed-ended research questionnaire to assess the level of awareness amongst officials of constitutional provisions on the status and roles of chiefs. The closed-ended questionnaire (Appendix 1) targeted a group consisting of selected government office bearers (civil servants only, not elected political officials) in national, state and local government. The survey was to identify the level of empathy amongst elites and officials in the government to recognise and to engage traditional authority systems in their roles as mandated by the policies. Enumerators were recruited to distribute and collected the responses for the structured closed-ended questionnaires.

Supplementary to this, but also important, was the structured symposium with the focus group (Appendix 2). This interchange was to probe on the suspected cluelessness, or intended design or oversight in policy formulation that excluded TALs from being incorporated in the structures and being effectively involved in decisions made and implemented at any level of government in South Sudan. The queries pursued responses from local government officials (civil servants) whom the researcher assumed to be competent in knowledge of constitutional provisions and competent in skills and expected to be fortified with a favourable attitude on the potentials of traditional structures in public administration and TAL legacy and their demonstrated transformational change leadership roles in mobilising rural communities during conflict and peacetime and participation in school and road construction.

The focus group discussion was designed to meet the requirement of what Turner (2010) calls qualitative interview design. In this structured open-ended method, questions were designed in such a way that allows respondents to give as much information as they would like. The interviewer raised probing questions in addition to ready-made ones. As the responses are uneven and differ in terms of length and content, coding of the responses present difficulties as suggested by (Turner 2010); on the other hand, the collective rich subjective data can help identify biases in the responses (Turner 2010:756).

The focus group discussions helped investigate the issues raised in questionnaires in more depth and breadth (Creswell, 2009; Erickson 1986:140). This approach assists in providing information about and capturing the participants' personal feelings and attitudes, which was found useful in analysing the data in this report.

Sample size of the study

The total number of respondents to the structured open-ended questionnaire with interviews (Turner 2010) was 43, consisting of 40 males and 3 females. The total number of participants in the focus group discussions was 17. All were males. Overlap of participants was allowed considering the wealth of knowledge and position in the targeted institutions.

The respondents were drawn from all the related fifty-eight (58) national institutions of the Government of South Sudan in Juba. In addition the Ministry of Local Government in Central Equatoria State and Juba County were targeted and successfully reached with questionnaires. Fifty forms were filled and collected. A total of 43 forms, equal to 86%, were correctly filled. Demographically, the respondents were 7% female and 93% male. Included was a member of the Fiscal and Financial Allocation and Monitoring Commission and a representative from the Specialized Committee on Legal Affairs in the National Assembly, a Director of Traditional Affairs in Juba County, Directors General of the South Sudan Local Government Board and a representative of the Ministry of Local Government and Law Enforcement of Central Equatoria State.

Review of primary sources

Several documents were selected for the review. These documents include policy documents which the Government of South Sudan deems important in empowering TALs and the local community in rural South Sudan. Documents included speeches by President Kiir, the SSTC 2011, and the Local Government Act (LGA) 2009. Also, included were each of the ten states' Transitional Constitution 2011 and the enacted COTAL Acts 2011 in five states in compliance with articles 165, 166, 167, 168 and 169 of SSTC 2011 and sections 6(2), 19(1), 19(2) and 19 (3) of LGA 2009.

The purpose of the review was to investigate whether the constitutional provisions contradict one another or whether the statutory provisions contradict one another or the constitution. Again, whether the policy documents are consistent or inconsistent with the constitution and statuary provisions and what is the reason behind any such inconsistency. Could that be by design, cluelessness or an oversight? Policy documents were further analysed to discover whether they contain strategies or action plans for implementation of the policy *Taking Towns to Rural Peoples* and/or the relevant laws. Particular focus was on the role of the executive and the legislature on the one hand and the TAL structures and systems on the other. The purpose was to review whether there are gaps in legal provisions or in implementation and to recommend plausible solutions for filling such inhibiting gaps either in terms of amendment or adding new provisions to the SSTC 2011 (or both) or in terms of new institutional reframing that could incorporate TAL institutions and encourage routinised consultative forums at national, state and local government levels in South Sudan.

Ethical considerations in the study

Participation in the study was based on oral individual consent, meaning it was necessary to ensure individual participants were willingly participating in the study. Participants were briefed that they were free to participate and that any of them had rights to withdraw from the study. The research questionnaire embodied an informed consent on each survey form provided. Respondents' names were kept confidential. Though some respondents requested being quoted with their names, the researcher did not name them in any of the findings. All related forms and analysis are kept in custody for the purpose of this research.

Methods of data collection and data analysis

This study used qualitative data analysis, which involves narration and description of the details in-depth. Data were coded and categorised into different themes and subthemes based on the constitutional issues addressed in the study. In other words, grounded theory of qualitative analysis was employed. This approach helps generate general issues and abstract theory of a process, action or interaction grounded in the views, opinions of the participants (Creswell 2009:13). According to Charmaz (2006) and Corbin and Strauss (2007), the advantage of grounded theory analysis is that it involves the use of multiple stages of data collection and refinement and the relationship of the categories of information collected from the respondents. Another advantage is that it constantly allows comparison of the data with emerging categories and theoretical sampling of different groups to maximise the similarities and differences in the information collected Creswell (2009: 14).

CHAPTER FOUR:
FINDINGS, DISCUSSION AND ANALYSIS

Sample size and demography of the respondents

All the related 58 national institutions of the Government of South Sudan plus the Ministry of Local Government in Central Equatoria State and Juba County were targeted and successfully reached with questionnaires. Fifty forms, equivalent to 98%, were filled and collected. A total of 43 forms, equivalent to 86%, were correctly filled. Demographically, respondents were 7% female and 93% male (see Figure 3).

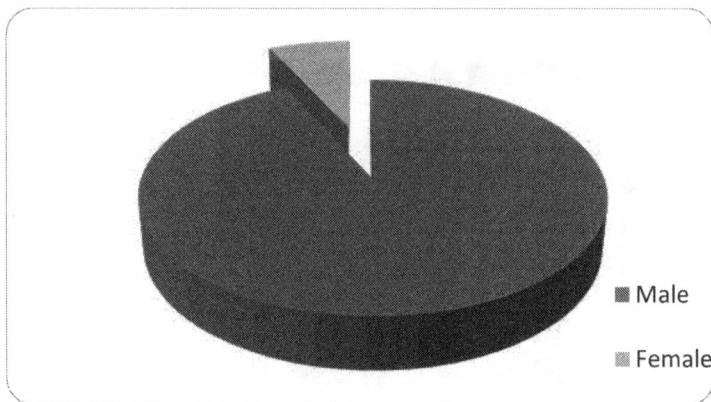

Figure 3: Demographics of respondents by gender

As for types of office bearers who responded, the following categories of people mentioned below filled in the forms (see Figure 4). The legal counsel and legal advisors constituted 40% of the total number of respondents. Any other category of respondent was below 5% of the total.

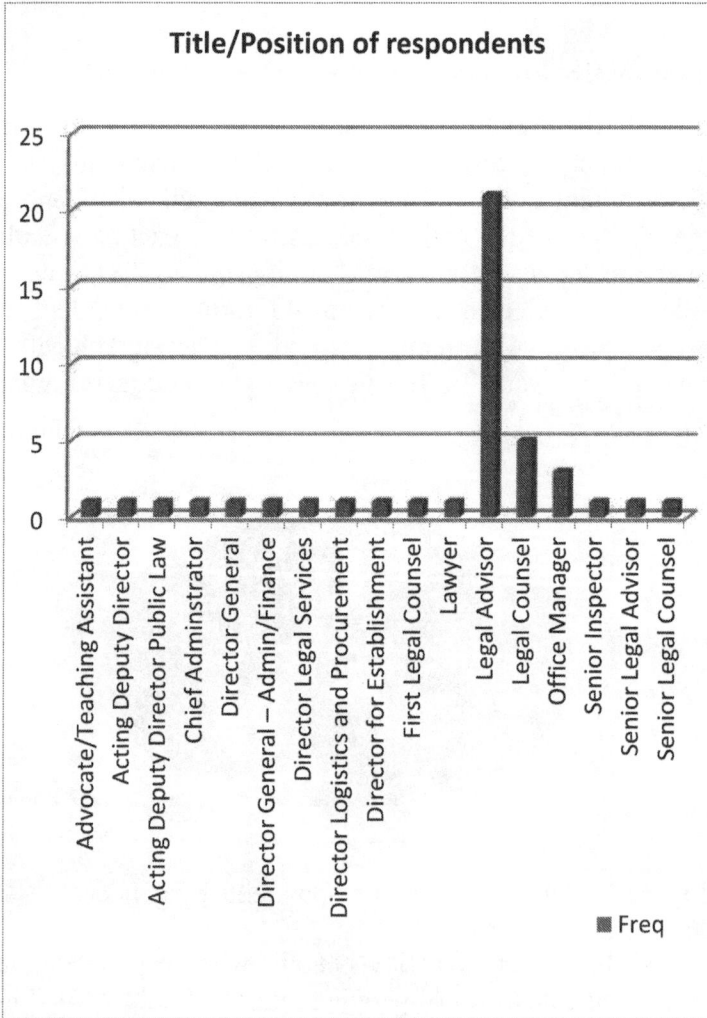

Figure 4: Respondents classified by profession

Findings from desk research

There were five findings as follows.

First, since its inception in 2004, according to (Deng 2013: 47) the policy of *Taking Towns to Rural Peoples* has suffered neglect. Evidence is the absence of an inclusive policy and lack of an implementation mechanism that should incorporate roles of TAL and their communities in a plan with an overall goal, specific goals, benchmarks, estimated inputs, timeframes and duties of specific institution(s) to implement identified benchmarks to implement the policy.

Second, there is no evidence of any annual budget allocation at any level of government put to finance the implementation of the policy. This is evident from the level of national budget allocation during 2006 to 2011. In that period the national budget consumed 74% of the resources while only 26% was reserved for all the ten states (Deng 2013: 50).

Third, in SSTC 2011, articles 50–53 on national government, articles 54, 55, 57, 59, 68, 83, 87, 90 and 93 on the establishment, composition and functions of national legislature, articles 108, 109, 110, 114 and 116 on the national executive and article 101 on the functions of the president are not responsive to SSTC 2011 article 168(2) on the constitutionally mandated roles of COTALs. At the establishment of state government, the composition and functions mandated under articles 162, 163 and 165 of SSTC 2011 are not responsive to article 167(1) and (2) on the recognition of the roles, status and mandated incorporation of COTALs.

Fourth, provisions on composition, establishment and functions of the executive, the national legislature and powers of the president contradict provisions on the type of government, guiding principles, economic goals, political goals, levels of government and devolution of powers mandated by SSTC 2011 articles 2, 35, 36, 37, 47, 48 and 49 respectively.

Fifth, the constitutional mandates on the establishment, composition and functions of national, state and local government levels are not responsive to the legal mandates of section 6(2) of LGA 2009 on the devolution of powers to local government closest to the peoples, and section 19(1) on incorporation of TAL systems into the three tiers of local government, section 19(2) on representation of the peoples by their TAL leaders in county legislature and section 19(3) mandating *boma* as a domain of TALs, where they shall perform administrative and customary roles. Instead there is an unconstitutional power usurped by local government in states and counties to appoint inexperienced young school leavers as *boma* administrators, which violates section 19(3) of LGA 2009.

Results/Findings from open-ended questionnaires

On questions about awareness of provisions on recognition of roles and status of TAL (see Appendix 2), 100% of the respondents answered *yes*. This indicates that all claim to be aware of legal provisions (Figure 3). It means zero per cent of them are not aware of the provisions.

This suggests these officials are potentially covering up what is likely to be their acute cluelessness. It is likely that some respondents did not want to expose their cluelessness about such constitutional provisions. Otherwise there is no reason why a civil servant would violate a legal provision on his/her roles. Further investigation is recommended. It is vital to identify the root causes of neglect or lack of adherence to provisions on mandated status, recognition, involvement and incorporation of TAL in the national, state, county, *payam* and *boma* government institutional framework and organisational culture. See Figure 5 below:

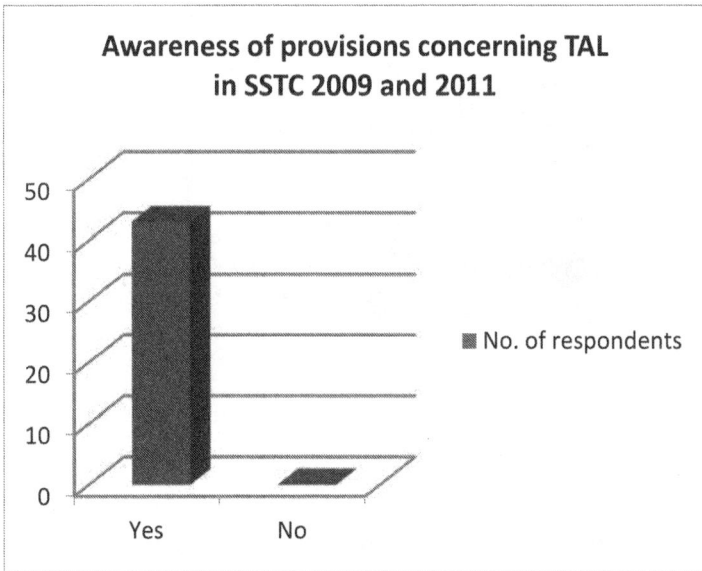

Awareness of provisions concerning TAL in SSTC 2009 and 2011

Figure 5: Level of awareness of legal provisions concerning TAL in SSTC 2009 and 2011

On the question of whether the respondents see the importance of TAL as an institution to complement the roles of the executive and legislature at national, state and local government levels (see Appendices 1 and 2), the result was 10% disagreed, compared to 90% of the respondents agreeing (see Figure 6). This finding is upheld by the results of the IRI opinion polls in 2011 and 2012 in South Sudan (see Appendices 6 and 7). In both opinion polls, respondents regarded the institution of chiefdom as the most favoured institution.

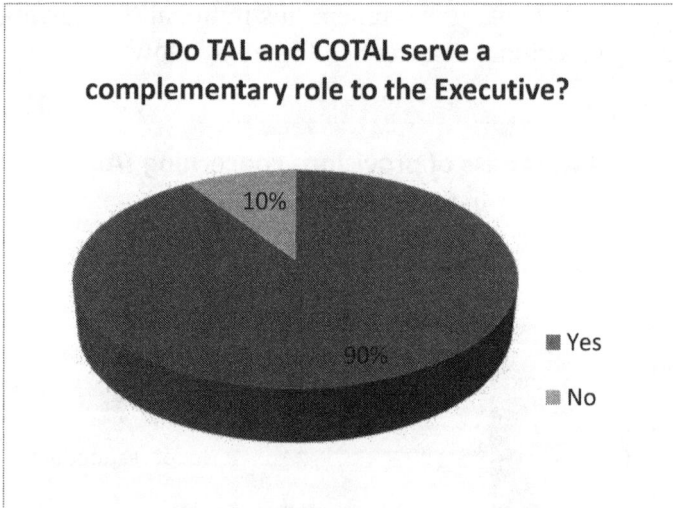

Do TAL and COTAL serve a complementary role to the Executive?

10%

90%

■ Yes

■ No

Figure 6: Level of agreement on whether TAL and COTAL complement the Executive

Another question asked was on the need to suggest additional legal provisions to ensure that provisions under articles 50, 51, 53 and 53, 54, 55, 57, 59, 68, 83, 87, 90 and 93, articles 108, 109, 110, 114, 116 and articles 101, 162, 163 and 165 of SSTC 2011 should be revisited to be consistent with articles 167 and 168(1) and (2) of SSTC 2011 and sections 6(2), 19(1), 19(2) and

19(3) of LGA 2009. The result was that 35% objected and 65% approved (See Figure 7).

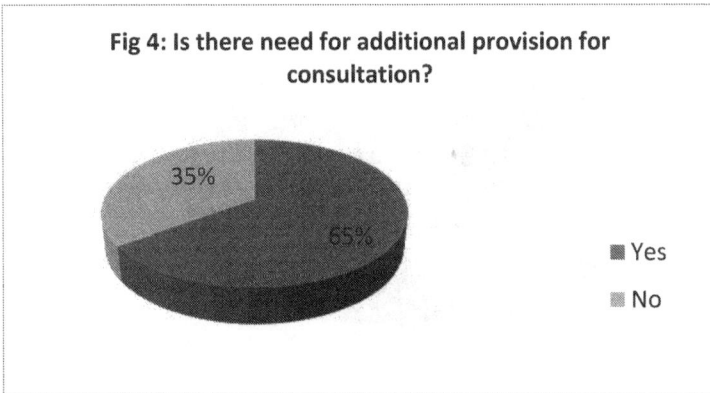

Fig 4: Is there need for additional provision for consultation?

Figure 7: The need to add further provisions

Results/Findings from focus group discussions

However, contrasting results emerged from a focus group discussion that was held on 10 May 2013 (see Appendix 2). The group consisted of 17 serving and former government officials. The Local Government Board in Juba hosted this discussion. Focus group participants responded with a unanimous yes (Figure 8) to the question on awareness of the existence of legal provisions mandating the status, roles and incorporation of TALs and COTALs as stipulated by the SSTC 2011 articles 167 and 168 and sections 6(2), 19(2) and 19(3) of LGA 2009. However, there is a need for caution. More investigation is needed to determine the level of knowledge of the legal provisions and to seek explanation why TAL systems are excluded.

Awareness of constitutional provisions on TAL

0%

Yes
No

100%

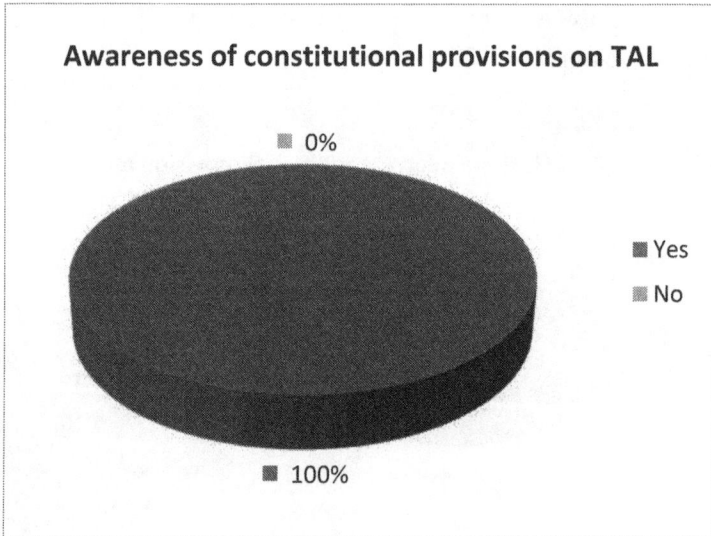

Figure 8: Level of awareness of constitutional provisions on TAL

However, during the discourse in the focus group discussion, one discussant vehemently opposed the suggested perception that the TAL systems and structures could supplement the roles of the executive and legislature at any level. According to this participant's view, TAL and their communities should be restricted to the village and their roles should be limited to customary courts. Another stringent respondent stated that TAL systems have no role in the decision-making sessions of the legislature, executive or administration at any level of government. Also it was noted in government publications reviewed that none quoted the president's speeches or policy statements directing the executive, the legislature and the party on the policy of *Taking Towns to Rural Peoples*. There was no evidence of any quote of constitutional provisions from the SSTC 2011. Above all it is observed that none of the above-mentioned publications contains a foreword by an SPLM leader or an ideologue of the party cadreship. It could be concluded that this variance could be blamed on lack of knowledge about the values of those policies. More importantly it might have been caused by inadequate supervision by the party of the executive and the legislature at national and state levels.

Results/Findings from familiarisation tour to South Africa, Botswana and Ghana

The Republic of South Africa has a National House of Traditional Leaders, including royal houses (see www.nhtl.gov.za), whose chairperson is Kgosi P.P. Maubane and Deputy Chair Kgoshigadi (lady chief). Each province has a Provincial National House of Traditional Leaders. The provincial or state laws prescribe the general composition of the council. Otherwise the community writes its own customary laws, which must be compatible with the national constitution in South Africa. In each District or Municipality there is a Local House of Traditional Leaders headed by a Kgosi-male/ Kgoshigadi-female. Kingship has been announced where there is a Kings Council under which 60% of members are appointed by the king and 40% elected by public. The hierarchy is the king, traditional leaders and headman. Under a headman there are 15 men and women as a committee to assist the headman spearhead the royal functions. Within the committee of the headman there is a committee for youth and another for women. Sometimes there are disputes that involve women's issues and cultural practices that are done by women and men. In terms of legislation, the principle traditional leader in that community has to be represented in the Municipality. Under legislation the kingdom is hierarchal.

Figure 9: His Majesty King Mpumalanga at King Makhosoke cluster Kgotla welcoming the delegation to the Provincial House of Chiefs, 18 January 2013

Acuil Malith Banggol

Figure 10: Women's cluster of Ndebele in Mpumalanga
Provincial House of Traditional Leaders

Unlike in Ghana and Botswana, there exists a
Congress of Traditional Authority Leaders
(CONTRALESA)[3] in the Republic of South Africa.
CONTRALESA continued in the post-apartheid period
to garner support for legislation to promote the roles of
TAL throughout South Africa
(http://www.sanews.gov.za/south-africa/dti-contralesa-
develop-rural-communities).

In South Africa, the system of local government, the
Department of Traditional Affairs[4], appoints experienced
and retired qualified former administrators and judges as
civil service staff to assist traditional structures,

---

[3] For further information, see http://contralesa.org.
[4] See http://www.cogta.gov.za/.

85

including clerks in the chief's office at village levels. Here TALs play greater roles in service delivery, engaging in interactive participation in development and monitoring of development programs through the community. Kgosi/ Kgoshigadi head public administration, allocate communal land to users and administer justice in customary courts linked to the national judiciary and magistrate courts at relevant levels.

An example of the vital roles of TAL in economic development is the success story of Royal Bafokeng Nation of Setswana people, who own communal land estimated at 1 000 square kilometres. The king initiated Royal Bafokeng Holdings as envisioned by a traditional authority in North West Province. They have the largest reserve of platinum in the world. Royal Bafokeng became famous during the FIFA 2010 World Cup, when it hosted the England team and hosted several games in its international sports complex.[5]

Briefings by host members of traditional institutions visited in Ghana, Botswana and the Republic of South Africa concur that traditional authority and its structures have demonstrated complementary roles of central government at a time when the latter is observed to hardly exist in rural areas. The judiciary system has incorporated customary courts so that citizens are free to engage the Customary Court and/or a Magistrate Court as defined by the procedures. In my opinion, traditional structures and systems are challenged to be responsive to

---

[5] See http://www.bafokengholdings.com/ and http://www.nytimes.com/2010/06/12/world/africa/12safrica.html.

demands by liberal citizenry, the roles and rights of women, youth and civic groups. The observations gained in Ghana, South Africa and Botswana demonstrated that chiefs, to maintain relevance, are progressively responsive to the ever-rising needs of modern development and globalisation.

In the Republic of Botswana, chiefs were instrumental already in the late 1800s in keeping the then Protectorate of Bechuanaland from being annexed to South Africa. A paramount chief, who later became the president of the independent Republic of Botswana, led the political struggle for independence of the country. As a result, TAL institutions continued to take the lead in modern-day Botswana. Chiefs enjoyed unlimited and undefined powers over their communities during the colonial period. In the then Protectorate of Bechuanaland, colonial administration exercised minimal control over community structures (Sharma 2010:2). The African Advisory Council, as it was designated in 1940, is now named Ntlo ya Dikgosi (National House of Chiefs) in Botswana. The Constitution of Botswana designates it is an advisory body to the bicameral parliament of Botswana. Appendices 4 and 5 provide details of the powers and functions of Ntlo ya Dikgosi in Botswana. Chiefs were already the chairpersons of the District Councils, whose membership included members of the community (Sharma 2010:3). Chiefs are represented in the Land Board in Botswana (Sharma 2010:4).

In Botswana a presidential commission known as the Venson Commission 2001 reported:

The role of traditional leaders in Botswana remains pivotal to the development process... Successful services delivery depends on the extent to which communities are engaged through their traditional structures of Kgosi [Chief] and Kgotla [District/Village House of Chiefs] where government officials at any level would consult with the community on matters that affect the community... . (Sharma 2010: 5–6)[6]

In Botswana, Dikgosi (chief) structures are responsible for the traditional legal system and development amongst their communities. Ntlo ya Dikgosi (National House of Chiefs) is an integral part of the lawmaking process. Bills on issues affecting communities and the traditional structures are tabled in Ntlo ya Kgosi before final legislation is made by the Parliament of Botswana (Appendix 4: Duties and House Business of Ntlo ya Dikgosi) and the Chairman of Ntlo ya Dikgosi (Appendix 5).

In Ghana, the then evolving anticolonial trend and democratic movement considered the perceptions of electioneering as the most valuable foundation for representing the peoples – the communities. The rising liberal perception of electioneering emerged as a challenge in the then process to relegate chieftaincy as nondemocratic. Chieftaincy institutions were mistakenly classified as nondemocratic institutions. This notion largely ignored the experience learnt from the colonial

---

[6] In South Sudan, article 166(6)(c) essentially mandates the same.

regime, which considered chieftaincy a necessary agent for the political administration of the colony. This notion of the undemocratic nature of chieftaincy dominated earlier stages of decolonisation in Ghana. Successive governments since 1951 would find chieftaincy unsuitable for governance in democratic Ghana (IDEG 2010: 14, 15). With the increased influence of movements for popular elective governance, the Watson Commission and Coussey Committee on political reforms could not salvage chieftaincy from marginalisation in Ghana (IDEG 2010: 14). However, two decades later the Akuffo-Addo Commission recommended chieftaincy as a significant tool in collaborative and widely owned rural public administration. Instead, the commission urged modernisation of the chieftaincy institution suggesting a need for educated chiefs (IDEG 2010: 21). As a result of such findings and recommendations and as mandated by the Chieftaincy Act of 2008, the current position of the chief is complementary to the government in Ghana.

In the briefings and publications presented to the visiting team, it was repeatedly stated that the structure and institution of chieftaincy is the single most visible governance institution in rural and urban Ghana today. In the modern-day nation-state of Ghana, there is a chief in every town and village complementing the role of public administration. The central government is not visible in most parts of rural Ghana (IDEG 2010: 21). Convincingly, Wiredu (1999: 39–40) concluded that the selection of a chief is democratic because it is always participatory through consensus.

During the visit to Ghana, the participants, including myself, learnt that the nation-state authority might not decide on matters that affect chieftaincy without consultation with the National House of Chiefs and with the Regional House of Chiefs and joint District Councils where chiefs are nominated as representatives. In Ghana it was found that their peoples at national, regional, district and village levels are selecting many former university professors, former bankers and ambassadors as chiefs or queen mothers. The visiting team was informed that the title of Queen Mother is given to a traditionally enthroned female chief, not a king's wife in modern-day Ghana. The chairman of the National House of Traditional Authority in Ghana is Professor Kwame A. Ninsin. It was observed that highly educated members of the community are enthroned at the Provincial House of Chiefs and District House of Chiefs. One example is the investment banker with an MBA from Yale University, Togbe (Hon.) Afede XIV. His Highness is the elected Permanent President of the Volta Region House of Chiefs. Togbe Afede is Director, Chairman of the Economy & Research Committee and a member of Strategic Planning & Budget at the Bank of Ghana. His Highness Togbe Afede serves as a member of many other boards in Ghana. In South Sudan evidence shows that educated chiefs and kings have been enthroned.

Interpretations of the findings

Firstly, in South Sudan, the SPLM-led government demonstrated severe disconnection to its vision, principles, goals and mission, especially in its goal of *Taking Towns to Rural Peoples*. This is evident in the stern absence of reference to SPLM policies and goals in all documents and publications so far. Secondly, in the literature review it was noted that a lack of responsiveness to SPLM policies amongst SPLM flag bearers responsible for publications is due to the suspected inadequate implementation of SPLM Second National Convention 2011 resolution number 9 and 10 on good governance and poverty eradication to be attained through the policy of *Taking Towns to Rural Peoples*. Lack of responsiveness by civil servants is blamed on legal gaps in provisions on the composition, establishment and functions of the executive at all levels of governance in South Sudan. So amendment is recommended to make these provisions compatible with constitutional provisions on TAL.

Thirdly, a lack of a code of conduct and disciplinary procedures meant that SPLM caucus members in the legislature and executive do not prescribe constitutional mandates as provided for in article 21(5) and article 38(3) of the SPLM Constitution 2008 to regularly relate to the SPLM General Secretariat for coordination and guidance on SPLM policies. Noncompliance with legal requirement is blamed on SPLM flag bearers not regularly communicating with the General Secretariat to ensure that executive and legislature at all levels adhere to articles 35, 36 and 37 of SSTC 2011, which are on guiding principles, political goals and economic goals of government in the country respectively.

The postcolonial state of South Sudan is a prototype of the Old Sudan, which was an archetypical colonial state similar to that of 1821 to 1956. This assessment is in respect to the existing relationship between the revolutionaries-turned-rulers and elitist public administrators on the one hand and the majority population and their TALs in rural South Sudan on the other. This in turn triggered a fragmented country, caused by exclusion, marginalisation, disharmony, hegemony and lack of trust, lack of mutuality and absence of interdependence amongst its rural and urban peoples. Renowned South Sudanese writer Dr Francis Mading Deng (1995) summarised the conflict of identity in Sudan in the title of his book *The War of Visions in Sudan*. Talking about disharmony and lack of trust between Sudan north and now independent South Sudan, Abel Alier gave the title *Too Many Agreements Dishonoured* (1999) to his book. What appears to have retarded the implementation of the policy *Taking Towns to Rural Peoples* and caused exclusion of TAL systems in governance is a broken promise.

In the then Old Sudan systems of governance, indigenous systems of governance, thoughts and desired connectivity were abridged and ridiculed as backward. Social networking amongst communities and within and between social strata was discouraged. The essence of power from the bottom up for collaborative decision-making processes and shared responsibility were prohibited so that self-efficacy amongst the indigenous peoples was smashed. TAL and the peoples in rural areas were excluded by the coercive and exploitative systems of successive governments in Khartoum (Malok: 2009: 10–33). Proclaimed rampant illiteracy amongst rural peoples was expended as a scapegoat to exclude TAL, though 'national governments' did not seek to overcome such limitations. Evidence to this effect is in responses by discussants as depicted in Appendix 2. In that, the assembled focus group participants were bewildered by questions suggesting recognition and involvement of TALs in the establishment, composition and functions of the executive and legislature at all levels of government as mandated by SSTC 2011 and LGA 2009. The discussants gave unreserved disagreement to such suggestions. During the discourse, every respondent claimed to be aware of constitutional mandates on the nature of governance and recognition of TALs. The question that arises is: If the civil servants have sufficient skills and awareness on mandated provisions, then how can inconsistent attitudes and practice by the participants (civil servants) be rationalised in not being responsive to constitutionally mandated provisions under articles 2, 5, 35, 36, and 37, 167 and 168 of SSTC 2011 and sections 6 and 19(3) of LGA 2009? It could be lack of relevant knowledge, attitudes and practices and a suspected individualism and curse of cluelessness amongst elites.

It is logical to suggest that there is a need for enforcement, guidance and coordination from the party and the political leadership to create the needed transformation and change as a culture. The results of focal group discussions revealed a need for a paradigm shift in governance in the country. There is need to orient civil servants and to inculcate in them new knowledge, attitudes and practices of good governance that could only be attained through interactive and inclusive decision-making processes involving rural peoples and their TALs as mandated by article 166 of SSTC 2011. Though it is true that civil servants should not be partisan concerning politics and in service delivery, they are expected to be knowledgeable, skilful, and professional and to abide by norms laid out in directives and laws enacted by the legislature that are responsive to constitutional mandates.

It is my contention that winning elections on a specific political agenda means that the governing political party is obligated to persuade, direct and coordinate with parliament to enact laws which permit implementation of the election agenda. Once such policies are legislated and enacted, civil servants, without resistance, should implement such policies under political advisorship of party cadres to ensure adherence to election promises. To reiterate, article 21(5) of SPLM Constitution 2008 mandates that SPLM caucuses in legislature and executive regularly relate to the SPLM General Secretariat at their respective levels for guidance and coordination. However, the irresponsive character demonstrated by SPLM flag bearers in the legislature and executive and amongst civil servants could be blamed on the suggested cluelessness caused by inadequate political training and non-existence of a triangulated leadership molecule (forum/team) oriented to enforce party principles. Therefore it is logical to conclude that lack of implementation of *Taking Towns to Rural Peoples* is attributable to the suspected collective institutional laissez-faire style of leadership (Bass and Riggio: 2006: 21) that befell SPLM institutional culture. To paraphrase Bass and Riggio (2006: 21) the result is deficiency in the expected roles of leaders to influence inspirational motivation and lack of idealised influence, intellectual stimulation and individual consideration and coaching to party rank and file and other followers in the country.

Strengths and weaknesses of *Taking Towns to Rural Peoples*

One example is the view expressed, in 2010, by the late Hero Kuol Deng Kuol, alias Kuol-adol (Paramount Chief) of Ngok Dinka, who lamented to me that *Taking Town to Rural Peoples* should not also bring the ills of towns. Kuol-adol cited cultural practice of forty days of expensive mourners' rituals in towns. He also decried the urban habit of wives and husbands not refraining from sex while the mothers were still breastfeeding, which is contrary to beliefs amongst rural Dinka. Kuol-adol feared the transfer of corruption and many unprincipled values and antisocial behaviours from towns that could negatively affect lives in rural areas.

During the Warrap State COTAL meeting (Tonj 2009), spiritual leader Dhoordit Ariik, of the Tonj Community, once challenged me on why elite persons and politicians would share a single roof in towns pretending to be in harmony while they pit rural communities against each other. Paramount Chief Dhoordit questioned the credibility of hypocritical calls for declaration of assets by constitutional post holders. Smilingly Dhoordit said:

> ...*monj* – you boy! ...When you, SPLA, left bushes, you did not have any assets ... How could you justify this sudden ownership of wealth to declare?

Dhoordit lamented that in rural areas the public always knows sources of wealth:

>...In towns issues are mixed up. ...That we do not like ... Such behaviours should not come with your proposed plans to take towns to rural areas ...

Views on essence and origin of TAL to be reassessed

In South Sudan, the essence, origin and hierarchy of paramount chiefs, executive chiefs, subchiefs, headmen, elders and religious authority are not artificial, as claimed by Hoehne (2008: 19). TAL systems were only recognised by the colonial administration to link colonial administration with colonised communities. In the culture I share, communities are named after their founding father, the godfather from whom they gain their spiritual leadership. Similar recognition of founding fathers was observed during our visit to the Republic of South Africa.

Acuil Malith Banggol

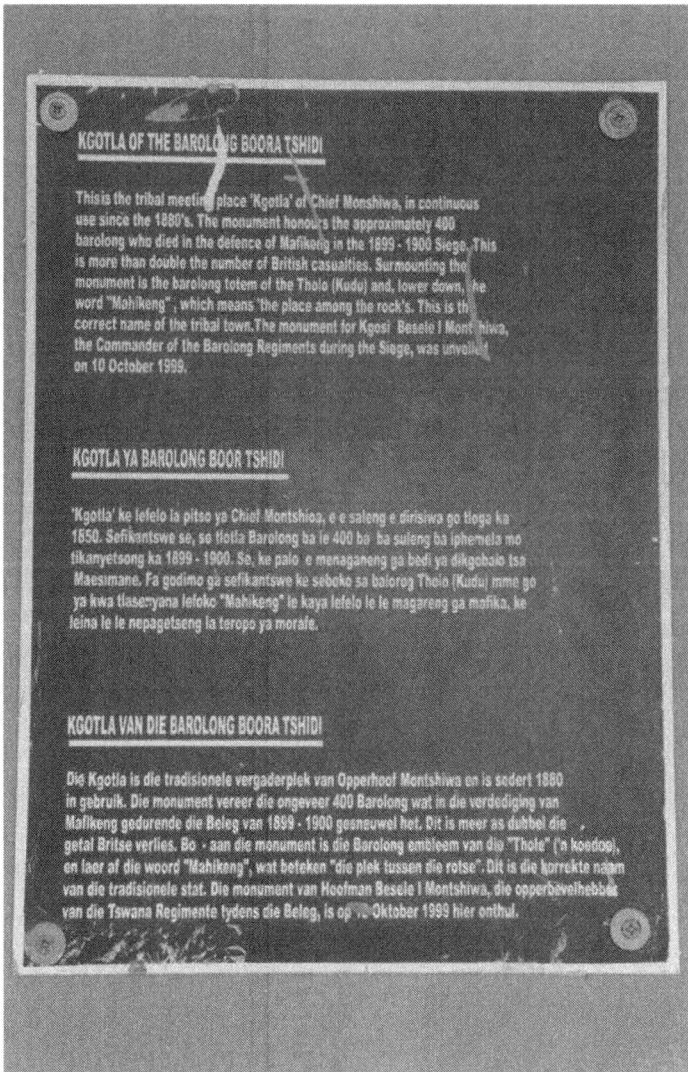

Figure 11: Inscribed history of Baralong Boora Tshidi community, Kgotla (chief's palace)

In South Sudan, the colonisers did not introduce TAL systems. They only renamed traditional structures, recognised and involved as TAL in the colonising administration. In fact colonisers reduced the status and roles of TAL because they were required now to seek recognition from and be accountable to colonising administration not to the rural peoples who enthroned them. The colonial officials' attitudes and practices were a personification of TAL as agents of exploitation. In separate works by Wassara (2007), Yom (2008), Kuol (2008), Arop (2012), Malok (2009) and Deng (2013), there is evidence that TAL resisted the colonisers' subjugation. Hoehne (2008: 14) quoted Leonardi (2007: 544) that colonial invaders humiliated, punished and coerced indigenous structures and their leaders to follow the will of the colonisers. Hoehne (2008: 15) contradicted himself because he ignored his own reference to Johnson (2003: 12), who admitted the existence of the kingdoms of Cholo and Anyuak. It is evident that some researchers comprehended royal systems, but failed to appreciate the mixed systems of elders, spiritual leaders, warriors and wise people and systems of traditional governance that existed amongst other communities in South Sudan. When colonisers asked for the focal point person from such communities, the response was that the highest spiritual leader appointed their nephews or influential, courageous and wise members to represent them. It is wrong to have disregarded those systems as absence of traditional governance structures. In recognition of the importance of TAL systems, new forms of traditional authority leaders were appointed by the British administrators as recommended by traditional governance but not created as suggested. This explained why British authority was respected. Acknowledging the use of coercive measures to subdue indigenous systems of governance indicates that TAL systems were in existence and were putting up resistance against capitulation and attempts to undermine their authority. Hoehne's work (2008: 15) supported similar traditional institutions elsewhere in Sudan as politically well-established families. However, Hoehne explicitly scoffed at non-feudalistic systems in South Sudan, using the word 'so-called' to refer to the liberal and traditional democracies of the egalitarian societies of Nuer and Dinka. Deng (2013: 9) concluded that prejudice concealed historical facts on the existence of the Kush Kingdom of Sudan, which was larger than Rome and its dominance over present-day geographical Egypt. Deng (2013: 9) quoted archaeologist Dr Timothy Kendal and Dan Morrison (National Geographic News: 18 June 2007), who determined that the Kush Kingdom's borders and influence reached the ancient Holy Land, the birthplace of Christ.

Essence of imprudent perceptions of status of TALs

The mental trap and prejudices of 'international experts' could be blamed for erroneous perceptions and translations held by indigenous South Sudanese intellectuals and politicians. They were educated and inculcated with reframed institutional culture and systems of pillaging, exploitation, exclusivity and marginalisation of the enslaving colonial state. South Sudanese elites were, as a result, influenced by the colonial masters' attitude of power distance and individualism, so they grab for self-enrichment. They formed 'national' movements, which struggled for a bigger say or to be included in government jobs with the colonial state, to plunder. Through the help of TALs and the rural peoples, elites succeeded in ousting the colonial masters. Unfortunately, elite revolutionaries-turned-rulers could not be dissimilar to the colonisers. The postcolonial nation-states and their officials followed in the footprints created by the invading nation-states, the colonisers. Freedom fighters-turned-rulers blindly applied the same oppressive rules to manage the postcolonial nation-states. I concur with the views of the late Ibrahim Nugud of the Sudanese Communist Party in Sudan, who concluded that during CPA implementation in Sudan 2005–2011, there was one country and two systems of governance. With the separation of South Sudan on 9 July 2011, two countries were formed, but with one system of governance. Both systems exclude and marginalise the peripheries, the rural areas.

Internal democratic procedures of TAL systems

Hoehne (2008: 5) quoted Branch and Mamphilly (2005: 12) stating that accession of powers to TALs raises the questions of both the internal democratic credentials of chiefs and of the possibility that seeds are being planted for intensified ethnic conflict. Tier and Dhal (2005: 66–105) expounded on how TALs through customary law courts, customary mediation and reconciliation are contributing to peaceful coexistence within and across communities in South Sudan. Colonial administrators explored opportunities of seasonal, cross-boundary peace meetings headed by TALs. Now in South Sudan many agencies engaged in similar peace and reconciliation processes rely heavily on TAL institutions. What is needed therefore is to take the institutions of law enforcement from urban centres to rural areas to back up the role played by TAL institutions in administration of justice and as a conduit of delivery of basic social services. Disarmament is the solution because rampant possession and misuse of small arms in crime has not only undermined the authority of TALs but also the authority of the budding nation-state in South Sudan. In contrast, the challenges caused by terrorist attacks could not warrant a call to abolish a nation-state system elsewhere. Instead, intelligence services and anti-terror and gun controls are agreed upon. It is, therefore, illogical to scrap TALs and not the nation-state because of the proliferation of small arms amongst rural youth. The solution is that this budding institution of nation-state in South Sudan should upgrade its law enforcement forces. More specialised anti-cattle theft mechanisms should be established and facilitated with skills and equipment to dissuade marauding youth in rural South Sudan. The executive in South Sudan should follow suit with the Judiciary of South Sudan, who appoint elected chiefs to preside over customary courts in *boma, payam,* county and town courts. During the familiarisation tour (January 2013) I observed that in Ghana, Botswana and South Africa the Ministry of Local Government and Traditional Affairs assigns experienced clerks to be office assistants and juniors to the elected chiefs who are appointed to head public service in districts. In South Sudan it is mandated by LGA 2009 section 6(2) on devolution of powers to local government closest to the peoples, and section 19 (3) mandates *boma* as a domain of TALs where they shall perform administrative and customary roles. Therefore, in my view TAL systems are well placed to complement local government roles in rural South Sudan to implement the policy *Taking Towns to Rural Peoples*. Local government should not appoint *boma* administrators from inexperienced members of society, now regarded as a distressing state of affairs. Local government should append to appoint elected chiefs as *boma* administrators as mandated by section 19(3) of LGA 2009. This is the practice today by the Judiciary of South Sudan, which appoints selected/elected chiefs to preside over the customary courts. Appointing junior members of the society who are usually selected from inexperience members to become senior rather than experienced, trusted and respected elected chiefs is interference in people's constitutional democratic choices in managing their affairs.

Though there is evidence that Hoehne explored this notion in his work, this researcher agrees with the view Hoehne (2008: 5) expresses when he quotes:

Simultaneously, (democratic) decentralization had increasingly been perceived as a way to improve overall local governance – in South Sudan as well as elsewhere in Africa. It is aimed at enhancing the participation of the local population in decision-making processes. Thereby it fosters transparency, accountability and responsiveness, and aids efficient and effective policy implementation. (Lutz and Linder 2004: 2)

There is much to be desired from Hoehne's (2008: 6) misleading quote of Mamdani (1996), who argues that: '...bifurcated in postcolonial Africa is a colonial legacy. It is based on the enforced division along ethnic/tribal lines and differentiations between rural and urban, as well as indigenous and other inhabitants of the colony...'

The situation in South Sudan is the opposite. Most Dinka and Nuer communities are members of immigrant communities of both sides and from other South Sudanese communities. Host communities through friendship and intermarriage incorporate immigrants across and within their social and administrative settings. In such societies, wanderers or new arrivals themselves and/or their first generations in their newfound homes have been inserted and selected as leaders. Empirical evidence of this is that it forms part of the belief and practice of this researcher. Clans with similar totem, *yath,* in Dinka or Nuer in South Sudan regard themselves as belonging to the same kinship family or clan – *dhien.* People of the same *dhien* traditionally could not, morally, engage in sexual relationship and were not allowed to marry one another.

The researcher asserts that many South Sudanese nationalities could easily trace their origin across administrative states, counties and *payams.* So the new developments of ethnic exclusion are artificial and could be removed by mutual interdependency and good governance where peoples are incorporated in their diversity in a mutually interdependent and collaborative decision-making process. TAL and rural peoples are dynamic in accordance to changing contexts and demands of globalisation. Mandates by SSCT 2011 on

Bills of Rights and consciousness could be legislated through a transformed desired reframed future state of routinised forums at national, state and local government levels. Sociopolitical, economic and cultural views should guide executive and legislature at all levels to include TAL and rural peoples in South Sudan as mandated by articles 167 and 168 of SSTC 2011 and LGA 2009.

Santschi 2012 concluded that:

...The World Bank and other major development agencies now emphasize the need to empower local community groups, including local government. That means giving them direct control over planning decisions and investment, while ensuring interactive participatory planning and accountability. Because public institutions in post-conflict environments are often weak, this approach is increasingly being used to build bridges between the nation-state and its citizens through their TAL systems. Due to their bridging role between society and the nation-state, the chiefs have a crucial role to play...

It is therefore recommended that such a paradigm shift is attainable through a reframed desired future state suggesting human resources development at all levels of government and traditional structures in South Sudan. Formal training and awareness campaigns are needed.

There is a need to have a National Day for TALs in the Republic of South Sudan. The purpose as suggested is to commemorate their legacy and achievements and to regenerate South Sudanese social capital through articulation of indigenous systems of governance, mutuality and thoughts and enunciation of a common destiny. It could be a way of integrating South Sudanese social systems of thought into modern spheres of life. Indigenous peoples led by their TALs and political leaders founded Republic of South Sudan on 9 July 2011. An example of favourable political will is the President Kiir's call, in May 2010, that:

> ...Our culture identification and development in all its forms must be unchained and facilitated ... through research ... to reach the same heights, as is the case elsewhere in our continent or the rest of the globe for that matter...

Therefore, I argue that policies on financing research in universities and research centres should be revamped as mandated by article 38 of SSTC 2011 on education, science, arts and culture. The peoples of South Sudan should set examples to leading nations of the world in expanding the annual celebrations of the International Day of the World's Indigenous Peoples to involve thanking TALs. The date of 9 August is annually observed to promote and protect the rights and achievements of the world's indigenous population. It is a reminder of how to protect traditional knowledge and traditional intellectual property rights and safeguard community land rights, promote indigenous languages, conserve environments and promote dialogue reflecting various indigenous multicultural values and to discourse with globalised cultures for justice, harmony, mutuality and collaborative prosperity for all. In South Sudan, therefore, civil servants and TAL should instead demonstrate a high degree of responsiveness or else it may be concluded that they form a dangerous dynamic resistance that is destined to fail the political agenda and that should not be left unchecked. Good governance should mean that political leaders should be held accountable to the election agenda. As such, civil servants should abide by constitutionally mandated and legally enacted policies and laws.

TAL institutions' potential transformational and change roles for prosperity

In the focus group discussion (Appendix 2) respondents cited different types of abuse of power. In one of the ten states of South Sudan it is alleged that an elected COTAL chair was dismissed and COTAL procedures frozen because of different views on accounting for COTAL money. State-level institutions unlawfully withheld resources transferred by the Local Government Board (LGB) and the World Bank to counties and funds to finance the elections of COTALs. There are claims that collections and remittances at county level fail to find their way to the government treasury as expected non-oil revenues. National block grants to states and local government are not transparently managed. Mandatory and trust levies and deductions for pensions leave no trace at all levels of government. These anomalies are fuelled by incompatibility and inconsistence of provisions on powers and functions of the executive and legislature at all levels. These anomalies violate explicit constitutional mandates on the constitutional term of office on recognition of TAL systems and on principles and goals of the government. TAL institutions should be empowered so that they are involved in all phases of any program that influences the livelihood of rural communities, and so that their priorities to develop economically are supported. Studies should look into alternative approaches that consider microfinance institutions which recognise non-banking systems through TAL institutions. Efforts could be made to use non-banking systems like livestock and traditional coping mechanisms as collateral supported by TAL institutions and customary laws. Block grants may fuel corruption. Incorporation, recognition and involvement of TAL institutions could enhance involvement of communities in decision-making and interactive participation.

Moyo (2010: 126–142) rightly suggests that the solution to underdevelopment and poverty in poor countries in general and in Africa in particular is to finance the trade and production sector. Moyo argues that aid grants fuel corruption and kill local productivity and trade. Moyo cited the successful example of banking in the un-bankable systems of community interdependence and mutual trust in Bangladesh. Other than mutual trust and interdependence there is no legal instrument between Grameen Bank and its borrowers. In rural South Sudan, traditional coping mechanisms are supported through lending and kinship mutuality. Wassara (2007) explained how TAL systems are effective in conflict management, and through kinship could effectively resolve disputes arising from payment and redistribution of dowry amongst relatives. The lesson learnt from the expanding and successful Grameen Banking[7] is that microfinance to 'poor' people has the capacity to create enterprise and economic growth in developing communities.

To realise this in South Sudan, there is a need to engage communities, community-based institutions and TAL institutions in governance and use the TAL system to prioritise and to ensure accountability. Within rural settings today, rural-based Development Committees, the chamber of commerce and the farmers union assist TAL authorities. Creating these rural settings is feasible. Youth are already taking the lead in such community-based organisations. It may only be lack of awareness or poor information that causes TAL systems to be regarded as obsolete and static. Claims that TALs are not educated are redundant and empty. University graduates and senior officials are now being selected and/or elected by their communities as chiefs or kings.

Taking Towns to Rural Peoples is needed so that rural peoples are empowered to engage in decision-making and as connectors to improve their livelihood and generate taxes to finance efforts needed to manage the peoples-centred nation-state. The rural peoples, through TALs, should be given a remedy to ease their sufferings. In the Republic of South Sudan, contradictions in legislation are glaring. These contradictions were observable in non-adherence to the provisions of SSTC 2011 articles 2, 35, 36, 37, 167, 168, 169, amongst others, and sections 6 and 19 of the Local Government Act 2009. These provisions attempted to

---

[7] See http://www.grameen.info.org.

portray that the liberated nation-state is not typical of a colonial state and surely not the same as Western-style democracies in sovereignty, sources of legislation and recognition, status of the peoples-led TAL institutions, and declared political and economic goals.

Suggested routinised consultative forums of COTALs and legislature in South Sudan

There is no teamwork and collaboration between the South Sudan Legislative Assembly and the Council of States on the one hand and the National Council of Traditional Authority Leaders as mandated by article 168(2) of SSTC on the other. The situation could be described as a disconnected system with no networking, as demonstrated by Diagram 1, which depicts how the three components are disconnected instead of complementing each other.

Fragmented present situation

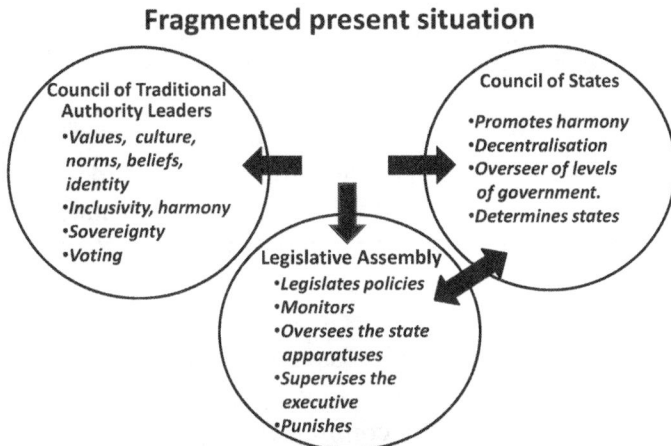

Diagram 1: Disconnected system of governance in South Sudan

109

The COTALs mandated by article 168 of SSTC 2011 is disconnected from the Legislative Assembly and Council of States. The rural majority headed by the COTALs, with an estimated 83% of population, dwell in the rural areas (SNC 2008), with elites estimated at 17% of the population (SNC 2008). The COTALs are not included in the processes of decision-making, legislation, planning, or implementation. From 2005 to 2011, the result was that resources allocation ignored the priorities of the rural majority. Over 74% of the annual budget was consistently allocated to the national budget and only 26% shared amongst the ten states (Deng 2013: 47). Diagram 1 illustrates that there has been little achievement in translating into the institutional framework and organisational culture the constitutionally mandated inclusivity that would ensure that communities and their community-based organisations were interactively involved in all phases of the decision-making process and implementation.

In the Republic of Botswana it was observed that there is a bicameral house. It is composed of the National Assembly and the National House of Chiefs, known as Ntlo ya Dikgosi (see Appendices 3 and 4). The functions of Ntlo ya Dikagosi as specified under the provision of section 85 of the Constitution of Botswana are guided by its conditional position as an advisory body with no legislative powers. Ntlo ya Dikgosi has three major roles. Firstly, as an advisor, it is to be consulted on bills affecting communal property, customary laws of the communal organisation or the customary courts. Secondly Ntlo ya Dikgosi is empowered to discuss any matter within the executive or legislative authority of Botswana which is considered desirable to take cognizance of in the interests of the community institutions and community organisations it represents and to make representations thereon to the president or to send messages thereon to National Assembly. Thirdly, it is to provide advice to the executive. As such, any minister may consult Ntlo ya Dikagosi in respect to any matter on which he or she desires to obtain the opinion of Ntlo ya Dikagosi, and for that purpose the minister or his or her representative may attend the proceedings of Ntlo ya Dikagosi. Ntlo ya Dikagosi renders its advice on traditional customary matters and any other matters referred to it by the government or the National Assembly. Ntlo ya Dikagosi is entailed to submit its resolution to the National Assembly after consideration of any bill referred to it.

In South Sudan, the situation may not afford the creation of another house but there is a dire need to have periodic consultative routinised forums similar to TALs at the Kamutu Conference 2004 and at Bentieu 2008. Dr John Garang and President Kiir consulted TALs on the CPA and the referendum respectively. The results of such consultative forums were encouraging.

To paraphrase (Hames 2007:181–208), today in comparison in South Sudan, Governors' Forums provide a process of a balanced bottom-up, top-down and lateral collective networking, listening and discourse, collaborative learning, deep thinking and strategic navigations that allows mutuality, trust and interdependence amongst conferees and subsequently their followers. This could be extended to the infrequent Commissioners' Forums in some states. Therefore it is proposed that routinised consultative forums of (1) South Sudan Legislative Assembly, (2) Council of States and (3) National COTAL would enhance a mechanism of decentralisation and *Taking Town to Rural Areas*. This is depicted in Diagram 2 below. But most important, such forums may allow national leaders to impart, as Bass and Riggio (2006: 21) suggest leaders of influence may do, '…inspirational motivation, idealised influence, intellectual stimulation and individual consideration and coaching…' to COTAL members and their followers.

Desired future for harmony and inclusivity

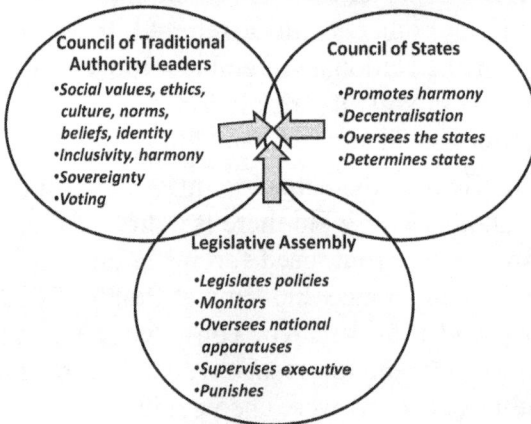

Diagram 2: Desired future state for harmony and inclusivity

It is logical to conclude that such an inclusive institutional reframe and organisational culture will be adopted as an annual or biannual consultative forum. Such a forum shall have a consultative role, as mandated to be added to the existing (a) National Legislative

Assembly and (b) The Council of States in accordance with the provisions of article 54 of SSTC 2011. This could lead to establishment of national forums as depicted in Diagram 3 below:

Desired situation: National House of Peoples

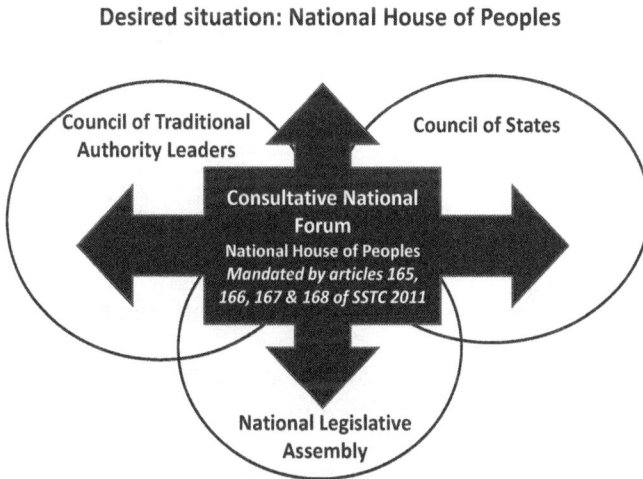

Diagram 3: Proposed routinised consultative national forum

A similar argument concerning disconnection is true of the governance situation at state levels in South Sudan. The fragmented situation pertaining to this is visualised in Diagram 4 below:

Fragmented present situation at state level

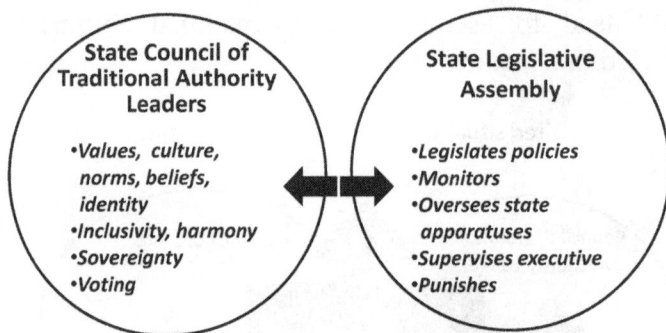

Diagram 4: Fragmented present governance in states

The proposed consultative forums at state government level are depicted in Diagram 5 below:

Desired situation: State House of Peoples

Diagram 5: Consultative routinised forums at state level

Such national and state forums could enhance economic growth because chiefs could be consulted and involved in decision-making. TALs could ensure that needed resources are adequately allocated to finance implementation of the policy *Taking Towns to Rural Peoples*. With that policy in place, it is logical to suggest that TAL institutions be granted a chance to ensure investment and employment in rural areas. This in turn is likely to curb rural–urban migration thus availing youth as a labour force in agriculture. Through such a collaborative leadership molecule (Flamholtz and Randle 2008: 60), TAL status could be recognised and involved in consultation on traditional customary matters and sustainable rural development as envisaged in *Taking Towns to Rural Peoples*. Again, the transformational leadership character of TALs in enhancing conflict mitigation processes could be explored through such forums at national and state levels. With peace and harmony through tranquillity and mutuality there could be a favourable atmosphere to enhance investment in agriculture, forestry, fisheries, livestock and trade. The impact of such transformation and change is intended to eradicate food insecurity and enhance access to quality education and health in rural South Sudan. In other words, empowering local communities as a constitutional mandate is very important and could be implemented similarly to successful stories of inclusive forums in other African countries.

To realise genuine and practical decentralisation and devolution of powers, four layers of governance are suggested instead of the present three layers of national, state and local government. An additional layer of TAL at *boma* level is needed as mandated by section 19(3) of LGA 2009. It could enhance interactive participation in identifying priorities, fulfilling duties, seeking rightful dues, provision of basic social services and contributing towards nation building, nation-state building and sustainable wealth creation for all and by all. Secondly, there should be local government (county and *payam*) to enhance coordination between the state authority and the *boma* administration. Thirdly, there should be the state government for the purpose of decentralisation. Fourthly, there should be the national government.

Benefits of collaborative leadership molecule and routinised consultative forums

The legislation and adoption of routinised consultative forums could create the chance for a process of a balanced bottom-up, top-down and lateral collective networking, listening and discourse, collaborative learning, deep thinking, strategic navigations and renaissance (Hames 2007: 181–208) (see Diagram 3 above). Such a leadership molecule and forums could serve as a bulwark against the tsunami waves of the ever and faster changing contexts and demands of a modern and globalised South Sudan. Such forums may enable a South Sudanese national culture to be built cemented by four dimensions as described by Hofstede, cited in the work by Bolman and Deal (2003: 249). These four dimensions are paraphrased to mean the following: (1) the shortcomings created by power distance shall be overcome, such that closeness amongst leaders of all tiers of governance institutions may help transformational leaders to influence, inspire and motivate followers, and through reciprocity the followers could help their leaders to clearly share the common national reframed views to eliminate the suspected curse of cluelessness, individualism and power distance; (2) uncertainty avoidance could be overcome through closed relationships so that a desired level of comfort and trust and mutuality is attained, within and between TALs and all levels of government in South Sudan; (3) suspected individualism is avoided, transformed and changed through a collaborative and collective leadership molecule, meaning that consensus and decision-making processes shall be the norm instead of the rampant, multicultural intolerance, winner-take-all mentality, lack of shared knowledge about other cultures and arrogance caused by cluelessness, and psychological control in decision-making processes; (4) the male–female balance as mandated by the SSTC 2011 could be adhered to.

Assumptions and suppositions on TAL systems in South Sudan

Tradition is about features and behaviours attributed to specific peoples influenced by their environs, customs and acquired knowledge and skills that shape their attitudes and practices. Examples are the American, Chinese and English traditions of coexistence with shared values, beliefs and symbols. Some researchers scoff at TAL systems and structures in South Sudan, but they recognise royal traditional systems of governance in Japan, the United Kingdom, Holland and Spain as being supportive of modern democracies. In South Sudan, educated TALs are now being enthroned. For instance, Executive Chief Manoon Ater Chol Guot of Noon Chol

Guot of Twic County is a graduate of the University of Juba. Amongst the Dinka Ngok of Abyei Administrative area are four university graduates. They are Kuol A. Makuec of Abior, Bagad M. Abiem of Man-Nyuaar, Chol Puur of Achaak, Arop Kuol Kon of Deel and Paramount Chief Bulabek Deng Kuol Senior Clinical Officer (Medical Assistant).

Figure 12: (L to R) Executive Chief Mangar Nhial Kon Anok, enthroned in the 1990s; Executive Chief Manoon Ater Chol (who holds a BSc Econ from the University of Juba), enthroned on 3 January 2011; and eldest Executive Chief Achien Yor, enthroned since 1965

Similar examples are *Reth* or King of Cholo who is a banker with a university degree. The late *Nyiiya* Agada junior and his successor *Nyiiya* Akwai Agada Akwai, King of Anyuak, were made to return from United States of America to be stooled by the visionary Anyuak people of Anyuak Land in Jonglei State. *Matat* (Paramount Chief) Alfonse Legge Loku Tombe, Chairperson of the COTAL in Central Equatoria state is a former laboratory technician from the University of Juba. Another example is also *Matat* Lazarus Ajanaba Lokule of Tindilo in Western Mundari of Terkeka *payam* of Central Equatoria state. Mata Lazarus was a member of legislature in Southern Sudan National Assembly 2006–2010. *Matat* Lazarus is a forestry graduate from the Shambat Institute of Agriculture in Old Sudan. *Bakindo* (King) Wilson Peni Rikito Gbudue, King of Azande, is a renowned, educated intellectual respected nationwide in the Republic of South Sudan. Madhol Lang Juuk-Amaldit is a graduate from Malakal Secondary School enthroned by Akuer Community of Twic County to replace his departed father since the 1980s.

So with a likely increase in access to education, nothing should prevent educated candidates from developing an interest in contesting elections for TAL in present and future South Sudan. In South Africa, Ghana and Botswana, former ambassadors and serving university lecturers are being enthroned as Kings or Queen Mothers. In the Republic of South Sudan the institution of TAL is challenged to be sensitive, responsive to and relevant in modernised society. TAL must be inclusive of necessary modernisation and include civic groups or modernised rural citizens of farmers, youth, women, professional associations, farmworkers labour groups and civic movements in rural South Sudan. TALs and their COTALs command the respect and sense of belonging of over 83% of the population of the people in rural South Sudan (see

Appendices 6 and 7). Undermining their constitutionally recognised status and functions would mean exclusion and marginalisation of the rural majority.

Hence, instead of calling for their abolition, nation-state institutions and international and local development agencies should review their views on the status and roles of TALs in rural South Sudan. What is needed is a rejuvenation of the culture of peace through empowering law enforcement agents and systems. TAL systems and structures need education to be engaged in processes of engendering inclusivity. TAL institutions as recognised and mandated by SSTC 2011 and LGA 2009 should be incorporate in the establishment, composition and functions in the legislature and executive at all levels of governance and be involved in all phases of setting the development and globalisation agenda in the modernised Republic of South Sudan.

Figure 13: *Nyiiya* (King) Akwai Agada Akwai, King of Anyuak in Jonglei state

Figure 14: *Bakindo* (King) Wilson Peni Rikito Gbudwe,
King of Azande, Western Equatoria State

CHAPTER FIVE:
SUMMARY, CONCLUSIONS AND
RECOMMENDATIONS

Summary

In summary, considering the valuable roles in history, the present and the future of modern South Sudan, the hypothesis of the study was that the most efficient and participatory mechanism to implement the promised goal of *Taking Towns to Rural Peoples* is through recognising the roles and status of TAL structures. The main objective of the research was to identify possible institutional restructuring and legal reframing to ensure that TAL institutions are incorporated in the establishment, composition and functions of the legislature and executive at national, state and local government levels as mandated by articles 166, 167, 168 and 169 of SSTC 2011 and sections 6 and 19(3) of LGA 2009. These research-specific objectives were to identify empirical evidence on the roles of TALs in enhancing interactive participation and wider ownership of the goal by the rural peoples. Policies were reviewed to identify suspected gaps and to propose solutions. Research methods used included a desk study of existing literature, qualitative and quantitative questionnaires and discussion, observation and familiarisation tours.

Despite favourable political will and the popularity of the anticipated goal, the findings confirmed lack of recognition of the status and roles of TAL systems and structures in South Sudan. This is blamed on lack of awareness due to acute cluelessness about the existing legal provisions. However, there was evidence of legal gaps caused by suspected oversight, if not neglect and exclusion, of TAL institutions in organisational design. This legal gap logically hinders involvement of TAL institutions in transformational leadership and change in decision-making process at national, state and local government levels. The interpretation is that such neglect and oversight has and may continue to cause the government not to benefit from the indispensable roles of TAL institutions in mobilising rural communities to realise a desired future state of *Taking Towns to Rural Peoples* in rural South Sudan.

Misleading viewpoints by some 'experts' that TAL systems are undemocratic, static and archaic institutions with no relevance in a modern nation-state attract criticism. Studies by many researchers confirm the view that TAL institutions play an essential role in service delivery, administration of justice, and in conflict prevention, mitigation and prevention. The findings of this research demonstrate that TAL systems and structures have already attracted university graduates in many African countries, including South Sudan, contrary to views that a TAL job is only for uneducated members of society. TAL institutions and systems of governance supported the liberation wars and the implementation of peace agreements. They could continue to be relevant and significant, similar to TALs during colonial times, in mobilising communities to build roads, schools and administration blocks. In South Africa, Botswana and Ghana, TAL systems have more visibility in rural areas than central government. They are in charge of public administration and administration of justice. In the Republic of South Africa, Botswana and Ghana, an enthroned TAL is approved to preside over customary courts and is appointed to be in charge of public administration by the Judiciary and Ministry of Local Government and Traditional Affairs respectively. In Botswana the National House of Chiefs makes up the second chamber of the National Legislative Assembly.

This study has shown that the Judiciary of South Sudan has incorporated enthroned TALs in administration of justice. Only the local government system in South Sudan is in violation of LGA 2009, SSTC 2011 and the political outlook as inspired in policy statements.

In conclusion

Any success of the proposed establishment, composition function and outreach of any modern nation-state institutions in South Sudan shall be determined by the level of inclusivity and recognition of the status and roles of TAL institutions as mandated by SSTC 2011 and LGA 2009. However, in South Sudan, civil servants and technocrats appointed and deployed by government suffer from cluelessness and professional individualism and have little willingness to adhere to legal mandates on the status and roles of TALs and their COTALs. Civil servants are not sufficiently informed and could not be more capable than the enthroned traditional authorities to credibly allocate national resources to finance the endeavour of *Taking Towns to Rural Peoples*. Civil servants could not be more accountable to peoples in rural South Sudan unless through TALs. The IRI opinion polls in 2011 and 2013 as shown in Appendices 6 and 7 provide empirical evidence indicating that traditional authority institutions are more trusted in South Sudan than many other national, state and local government institutions suggested in the polls. The accusation that rampant small arms in rural areas have weakened the capacities of TAL is due to limited disarmament and is exacerbated by the limited capacities of law enforcement agents to dissuade potential culprits.

Furthermore, the lack of adherence of civil servants to mandated constitutional mandates and policy directives that was identified could be attributed to the disconnectivity and disharmony in the ruling party, the SPLM. This creates a phenomenon where the party is not able to fulfil its election manifesto and mandates due to inadequate supervision, coordination and guidance. This in turn is caused by major three challenges. Firstly, the National Secretariat is not fulfilling its mandated roles under article 22 of SPLM Constitution 2008, which demand that the National Secretariat translate policies into programs. Secondly, the National Secretariat suffers from inadequate cadreship training and an inadequate induction mechanism. Thirdly, though SPLM members in the executive and legislative caucuses and SPLM leagues are mandated by article 9(17) of SPLM Constitution 2008, they never receive orientation or induction. Subsequently SPLM caucuses are not responsive to article 21(5) of the constitution, mandating them to frequently relate to the General Secretariat for coordination and guidance at their relevant levels in states, counties, *payams* and *bomas* in accordance with articles 35(8) and (9), 45(8) and (9), 55(9) and (10), and 64(9) and (10) respectively. SPLM Chairman Kiir's directives on 15 November 2013 on mandated SPLM intuitional connectedness and coherence merit responsiveness.

Comparatively, central governments in Ghana, Botswana and South Africa are more advanced than the Republic of South Sudan in outreach and infrastructure, but have extensively incorporated TAL institutions in the judiciary and public administration, and TAL systems are recognised and involved in processes of resources allocation and service delivery. But South Sudan elitist institutions are bent on excluding traditional authority systems in policy promulgation, decision-making processes and implementation phases. Such exclusion is taking place despite constitutional mandate, historical legacy and political will that support and recognise the roles of TALs, who have demonstrated their significance in the past, the present and in the foreseeable future in South Sudan.

It could be established that there is logic in the hypothesis proposed here that TAL institutions in the country, if engaged through reframed institutional and legal framework, could promote social protection and enhance social and political capital around government roles to efficiently, effectively and in a timely way implement the goal of *Taking Towns to Rural Areas*. In so doing, the roles of TAL institution are indispensable within the social context in implementing the mandates of SSTC 2011 article 181(2) on the establishment, composition and function of the Fiscal and Finance Allocation and Monitoring Commission. The commission could engage the social and institutional factors of the national COTAL, the state COTAL and individual TAL institutions to fulfil its constitutional mandates under article 181(2)(a) is to ensure and monitor any grants throughout all levels of governance in the country. Article 181(2)(b) is to guarantee appropriate sharing of resources at state, local government and *boma* levels. Article 181(2)(c) is to safeguard transparency and fairness in the process of allocation and implementation. Article 181(2)(d) is to monitor utilisation of grants, and article 181(2)(e) is to engage TAL system on issues that interest the local communities.

Recommendations

The facts demonstrate the correctness and continuing relevance of the findings of this research. Recommendations made now in 2016 on the relevance of TAL institutions concur with recommendations made on the same in 2013/2014, when the study was first conducted.

It is clear that President Kiir's policy statement (Appendix 9) supports the findings, argumentation and recommendations on the roles of TAL institutions in achieving the goal of *Taking Towns to Rural Peoples in South Sudan*. This is evident in the dynamics of the ongoing political outlook and calls for inclusive, just and good federal governance for prosperity in multinational South Sudan.

In the opening speech at the Consultative Workshop for Establishment of the Ministry of Federal Affairs, on 15 November 2016, First Vice-President General Taban

Deng Gai read a message from President Kiir explicitly expressing political will in favour of federalism: 'As the President of the Republic of South Sudan, I am committed to the principles and ideals of federalism... [T]he hierarchy of the institutional framework for South Sudan, starts with boma, payam, county, state and then national government...'. Preceding developments support the same desire for establishment of a free, inclusive, social democratic and prosperous federal South Sudan devolving more federal powers to *boma*, which is the closest constituent unity to the peoples. This newly adopted vision emanated from a statement of goals of the Agreement on the Resolution of the Conflict in South Sudan (ARCISS) 2015, which was signed on 17 August 2015. The agreement stipulates that the constitution-making process shall be based on two principles (ARCISS, Ch. IV: 1) 'Supremacy of the people of South Sudan' and 2) 'Initiat[ion of] a federal and democratic system of government that reflects the character of South Sudan in its various institutions [which] taken together, guarantees good governance, constitutionalism, rule of law, human rights, gender equity and affirmative action'.

Earlier on, there was expression of a similarly consistent political outlook. President Kiir stated on 15 August 2016, on the occasion of the inaugural opening of the Transitional National Legislative Assembly (TNLA): 'I am calling here for the establishment of an inter-political all South Sudanese Public Council. Experts from all fields, ordinary citizens from all walks of life, nationalities representatives, young professionals and students will convene twice a year and engage in discourse on the direction of our country. This will not eliminate differences but will create forums and mechanisms to debate in a civil and open way'. This call supports the establishment of a National and State Council of Traditional Authority Leaders as mandated by article 167(1) and (2) of SSTC 2011. This is demonstrated in Diagrams 2 and 5 respectively.

Proposed strategic framework:

This study has provided empirical evidence confirming that non-recognition of the status and role of TAL institutions and their exclusion from all levels of government in South Sudan is deliberate by design. This may potentially be a policy oversight, but is made worse by an apparent lack of awareness of existing constitutional mandates.

The envisaged goals to address these anomalies include:

- publishing the findings to enrich literature on the roles of TAL in South Sudan to encourage more research and to provide knowledge to stakeholders
- assisting TALs and the COTALs formed in states to engage stakeholders to support implementation of COTAL Acts in their states and to engage them for formulation, legislation enactment and implementation of a national COTAL as mandated by article 168 of SSTC 2011
- engaging COTALs and TALs to lobby for implementation of articles 166 of SSTC and section 19(3) of LGA 2009
- empowering COTALs to lobby the youth, women, civil society and the government and donor

community to expedite realisation of the desired future state (Simonson 1997: 54) of *Taking Towns to Rural Peoples*

- empowering COTALs at state and national levels to engage in submissions on needed legal provisions and reframed institutional structures through the ongoing National Constitutional Review Process
- engaging COTALs at all levels to suggest and lobby for enactment of policies on institutional framework and organisational culture that may enhance the role of TAL institutions
- allowing COTALs and stakeholders to lobby for upgrading the LGB to be the Ministry of Local Government and Traditional Affairs in South Sudan.

Suggested actions:

- Make presentations to the executive and the legislature at state and national levels.
- Make presentations to TALs, COTALs and stakeholders.
- Encourage COTALs in the states to lobby for formation of a national COTAL to engage all actors locally and at state and national levels.
- Seek funding to support activities.
- Educate and encourage TALs in the states to form their SSACOTAL similar to the COTAL of South Africa (CONTRALESA) and the East Africa Association of Traditional Authority Leaders.
- Seek funding to publish this report to enrich the literature.

CHAPTER SIX:
ENVISIONED TWINING OF
GOVERNANCE IN SOUTH SUDAN

Introduction

This chapter is a later addition. It takes the opportunity to explore existing constitutional mandates and the favourable political will as dictated by changing contexts and demands in South Sudan. The chapter advocates for concrete actions that could enhance TAL roles in enhancing administrative, governance and accountability roles through the envisioned process of *Taking Towns to Rural Peoples* in South Sudan. This chapter suggests programs built on opportunities to further promote awareness and to make a timely call for suitable actions to institutionalise constitutional mandates that incorporate the roles of TAL institutions at all levels of government in South Sudan. This is judged from lessons learnt as documented in many studies on TALs. Since the colonial era, the British Administration in Old Sudan, followed by the successive regimes that came and went in Khartoum, there was a system of indirect rule. TALs were made responsible and authorised to maintain peace and tranquillity within their communities. TALs were used to administer customary justice. The government, to mobilise communities to support schools and the building of infrastructure, relied completely upon TALs. By June 1947, TALs participated in dialogue, through the Juba Conference, on the political future of the Southern Sudan. During the 1983–2004 armed struggle in South Sudan, TALs emerged to fill the then defunct public administration. More importantly, TALs supported human and material mobilisation. With the successful founding of the Republic of South Sudan in July 2011, the constitution mandated incorporation of TAL roles and COTALs in the sustainable establishment of inclusive, just and good governance at all levels. Therefore, these notes explain how a pragmatic twining between the political nation-state and the existing societal nation-state of TCFSs of governance, in *boma* constituent units, could enhance consultative dialogue amongst the nationalities. Also, the process could enhance collaborative dialogue, learning and consensus between the government and the rural majority led by TALs and TCFSs. Recognition and involvement of TALs could enhance accountability, transparency and inclusive good governance.

Earlier on, until 2013, some eight states out of the then ten states of South Sudan were supported by the Swiss government to enact the state COTAL. It is imperative to build on this successful program to cover all the states. The same State COTAL Act could be adapted by the newly established states. The priority now is to translate each state COTAL into the envisaged institutions to fulfil the popular demand and the constitutional provisions mandating recognition, incorporation and involvement of TAL institutions in all levels of government in multicultural South Sudan.

With eruption of hostilities in December 2013, there was a halt in the process of helping the states to translate the COTALs into an institutional framework and organisational culture. However, it is now opportune to explore the contexts with implementation of the ARCISS

2015 and the formation of the Transitional Government of National Unity (TGoNU) 2016. Some donors have shown interest. Several forums have been facilitated. The recent Kuron Village meeting of chiefs suggests the importance of empowering TALs. During the recent Kuron Village meeting, the chiefs demanded such forums to be able to dialogue on peace and the healing process. There were voices amongst the chiefs asking for a forum with the government and parties to ARCISS 2015.

Some states, like Aweil state, have invited Policy Advocacy & Strategic Studies (PASS) consultants to help the state authority to adapt the State COTAL Act and adopt TAL institutions. Hence, these concept notes have been developed to give wider information and justification. More literature was able to be accessed in the course of research for this book. More detailed programs are being designed in collaboration with targeted states to implement the State COTAL Act. In that, PASS consultants have embarked on mobilising the necessary expertise and collaborative network to engage the stakeholders.

Background and justification

PASS consultants add their support to the wisdom of supporting continuous research on the roles of TALs. But it is now timely to have more accompanying actions to institutionalise the roles of TAL institutions at all levels of government. This could ensure inclusive, just and good governance in the country. Above all, such support could enhance the timely, sustainable and widely owned process of implementation of peace, reconciliation and peaceful coexistence. Delays to enforcing these legitimate legal provisions could create apathy associated with lost opportunity. Lack of action could cast South Sudan into irreparable social disharmony and cause deep wounds. There is a genuine fear that, with non-action, elites in the government, suspected of suffering from cluelessness about the mandates on the status and roles of TALs, could annul the mandated roles of TAL institutions. The goal of this publication is to engage the government, TALs and stakeholders. This move could enhance the roles of TALs in effectively and efficiently contributing towards reconciliation, remorsefulness, peaceful coexistence and the development of the modern nation-state of South Sudan. The proposed institutional framework and organisational culture are founded on practical experiences in other African countries, extensive research, and logical recommendations on the indispensable roles of TALs in South Sudan. This research confirms the necessity of TALs in enhancing mutuality, unity in diversity, and inclusive, just and good governance amongst the 72 nationalities in South Sudan. Such institutions could allow the timely realisation of existing processes of twining governance in South Sudan. This is also anticipated to augment the benefits of the exercise of routinised consultative forums amongst communities and their government. Such institutionalisation, if allowed, should prove to support two-way communication between the political nation-state on the one hand and, on the other, the TAL institutions mandated by the constitution in accordance with the provisions of article 166, 167 and 168 of SSTC 2011 and section 19(3) of LGA 2009.

Perceptions of the envisioned twining model

Model 1, below, is a rephrased perception of a model by Mayen (2013: 145), presented in his book *The House of War Africa*. This model by Mayen expounded on the hypothesis of a necessary social contract between the communities and the modern nation-state in African contexts. The model explains how such a social contract is being eroded. In his proposition, Mayen explained that chronic political instability and recurrent civil strife are mainly manifestations of the suspected erosion of the social contract. Mayen explained that, though at a liberation stage, such a social contract led to collaborative efforts to liberate the nation. Mayen concluded that the hypothetical post-independent African governments excluded and marginalised the 25 communities of their 'tribes', causing societal anxiety and disappointment. This makes each of the communes' collaboration prone to negative mobilisation by frustrated politicians whose interest is fomented and who manipulate conflict between the political nation-state and their communities. The disgruntled politicians then opt to mobilise the disappointed communities to fight for power sharing in the centre. Hence, the logical suggestion is to restore harmony and social cohesion and the social and political contract. This is to repair and to rejuvenate trust through twining between the political nation-state on the one hand and the TCFS and its TAL institutions on the other.

The rephrased Model 1 depicts the South Sudanese political nation-state as being made up of several administrative states. In the Republic of South Sudan, this establishment is perceived within three geopolitical greater regions. These are the Greater Bahr el Ghazal, Greater Upper Nile and Greater Equatoria. Close scrutiny of the rephrased model suggests obvious dynamics. In that, the changing contexts and demands reveal that some administrative states coexist within a geopolitical greater zone. Furthermore, within each administrative state there is the collaborative existence of several numbers (#) of TCFSs of governance. Each TCFS is headed by a TAL as a head of a clan (*wut* in Dinka), with an existence genre comparable to a sovereign nation-state. Each TCFS is customarily and statutorily identified with land, space, governance and a people (commune). Led by a TAL, each TCFS is mutually recognised with a specific form of economy and a standing legion of youth-*Monyomiji, Ric, Rem, Buulok and others*, amongst many South Sudanese nationalities. The youth are arranged to enforce territorial boundaries, customary belief, norms, values and practices. These are customary mechanisms and norms, mutually observed to protect life, property and community-owned natural resources.

In South Sudan, TCFSs are shortly to be recognised as sovereign nation-states because they lack international recognition by the United Nations and do not operate a diplomatic mission beyond their frontiers other than through marriages and responsive mutuality and peaceful coexistence. Even if they do not qualify to be considered as sovereign nation-states, each TCFS enjoys jurisdiction and belongingness cemented with considerable social contract and responsibility, patriotism and loyalty through mutuality within and amongst the inhabitants of a TCFS. The joint political nation-state in South Sudan could learn from the valuable mode of collaborative existence in each of the TCFSs, popularly referred to as chieftaincies or kingdoms. This could rejuvenate social responsibility and build a South Sudanese nationhood and remorsefulness united in diversity. In South Sudan, each of the TCFSs could be identified with kinship and mutual traditional coping mechanisms with duty-bound and compelling collaborative social responsibility, accountability and sacrifice for a common cause. Recognising the status and roles of TAL institutions could stretch this noble collaborative coexistence and establishment to building South Sudanese nationhood, commonality and unity in diversity.

Twining model of federation via *Unity in Diversity*
Political nation-state and societal nation-state
A case for social & political contract in South Sudan
Rephrased from Mayen (2013: 145)

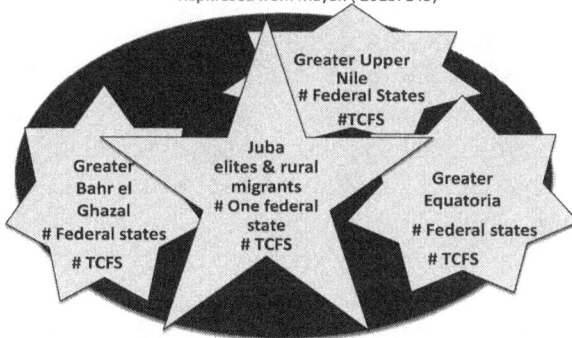

Diagram 6: Model 1 – Twining model

Obviously, in each geopolitical region there are numbers of administrative states that may increase or decrease as the situation demands. Each of these administrative states is made up of a number of TCFSs. In South Sudan, the challenge is that intellectuals, economic migrants and displaced community members from these TCFSs to urban areas would opt to explore the national victory while unjustly excluding and demonising TCFSs. In what seems to be a spillover from colonial governance, elites have opted to craft a nominal and exclusive nation-state delinked from TCFSs. This has resulted in exclusion and marginalisation of the rural majority. The bitter truth is that today's political culture in South Sudan is characterised by a negative norm. A sizeable number of South Sudanese intellectuals and their mushrooming political parties demonstrate a disturbing lack of clear political outlook. These wickedly crafted political parties become like political curtails. They serve the egoistic and individualistic attitude of their founders who have the demonstrated goal of pressuring the government and the international community to ask for a quick fix, known as power sharing. Most of the town dwellers come from diverse cultural and chauvinistic groups who opted to migrate to the centre of Juba city, the political capital of South Sudan. Experience has shown that in urban areas the immigrant elites tend to live and collaborate as a community to customarily resolve kinship and marriage divergences. But experience has also shown that elites and rural–urban immigrants have established systems of governance that exclude the rural majority in the form of TCFSs led by TALs. Bizarrely, in most African countries today, like South Sudan, the egoistic elites would frequently exploit their status as social gurus to mobilise their communities to fight the government to pressurise for constitutional assignment known now as power sharing. In the unlikely situation that these jobism dreams are not attained, the alternative is that the losers of such chauvinistic attempts would opt to mobilise their communities to take over power in the centre or to negotiate for power sharing. TAL institutions are major actors and necessary connectors between communities and with the modern nation-state for accountability and mutual trust to insure inclusive, just and good governance for all.

Examples of successful twining governance in the world

In the Botswana model, the Kgotla (The National House of Chiefs) is the second chamber in the National Legislative Assembly. This is structured at governance levels such as the National, Provincial and District Houses of Chiefs incorporated by the constitution as part and parcel of the Botswana public administration and the administration of justice and land. It is similar to national and state COTALs in South Sudan as mandated by article 167 and 168 of SSTC 2011 – see Diagrams 1 and 4 above, indicating the disconnected state of affairs of legislation at national and state levels. Such disconnectedness could be resolved through the proposals in Diagrams 3 and 5 above.

The Ethiopian peoples' federalism is mandated by the constitution to recognise and involve each of the 75 nations, nationalities and peoples of Ethiopia in the House of Federation of the Federal Democratic Republic of Ethiopia. It is the second house of the Ethiopian parliament that ensures mutuality, unity in diversity and peaceful coexistence. This could be adapted to be a routinised consultative forum practised annually or twice annually, to be named the House of Peoples as depicted in Diagrams 3 and 5.

In South Africa and Ghana, similar to most countries in the southern African Region, there are national, provincial and district Houses of Chiefs mandated by the constitution. TALs (chiefs, queens and kings) and their roles are incorporated in public, administrative and judiciary roles and land issues and as a mechanism to involve communities and community-based organisations.

Swiss federalism, consisting of 26 cantons with 4 linguistic divisions (Italian, German, French and Romansh) and two major faiths (Catholic and Protestant) has created social harmony and a nationhood based on unity in diversity. Democracy is exercised through direct democracy via referendums subject to the law.

The forms of federalism practised in India and Indonesia are founded on mutual recognition and unity in diversity amongst hundreds and thousands of TCFSs of governance similar to those in South Sudan.

Such twining is in existence in the Republic of South Sudan. It should be recognised and strengthened to achieve inclusive, good governance and unity in diversity. Twining through inclusive governance is mandated by article 1(4) of SSTC 2011, which recognises and embraces all the homelands of its peoples. It recognises the dignity of each nationality, culture, language and faith. Article 2 of SSTC 2011 explicitly mandates sovereignty to be vested in peoples' democratic and representative institutions, which includes TAL institutions as mandated by the constitution and the law. The recognition of communities and cultural groups is explicitly mandated by article 33/SSTC 2011 under the right of cultural communes. This is also mandated under 36(4)/SSTC 2011 as a political objective to command national unity in diversity and social cohesion amongst the 72 nationalities in South Sudan. Such readings justify the proposed tricameral consultative forum as demonstrated in Diagrams 1–5 above. This envisioned twining is mandated in South Sudan under article 166, 167, 168 and 169(3) of SSTC 2011 and under subsidiary policies of LGA 2009, especially section 19(3) of LGA 2009 on the status of *boma,* that is TCFSs, under TALs.

Some empirical facts about TCFSs and TALs in South Sudan

In Santschi's work (2010), it is reported that chiefs play a key role in local government in South Sudan. These roles include delivery of services and acting as connectors between the political nation-state and the TCFSs. Chiefs have been identified as having the ability to foster development programs. In that respect, Santschi concluded:

...Chiefs play an important role in community life in the young nation of South Sudan. They provide an array of vital services, from mobilising people for community projects to adjudicating disputes and administering customary law. Sometimes criticised as being an unelected group of old men, they will nevertheless play a vital role in South Sudan's

141

steps to building viable, effective, local government institutions...

Concurring with Santschi's findings, Leonardi et al. (2011) agreed that:

The chiefs' courts presumably will continue to be one of the major justice providers in South Sudan during the next decade. Due to the customary law's flexibility and mutability, these courts are able to adapt to social change...

Schomerus (2015: 14, 17) quoted a respondent in the Ezo and Tambura counties that: 'The very issue is we want to maintain our cultures and norms; we cannot fully do that with the government'. There was a clear sense of stronger local political organisation, which would help to stand up against unpopular government decisions: 'Outside town the land is solely under the community's control. If the government is to invest they have to ask the community. From the community, the chief is the key person ... Nobody is helping apart from [the] chief; the only government looking after us is [our] chief...' A Picher Polls Results conducted by the IRI (6–27 September 2011) revealed TALs were leading in opinion of the respondents. The importance of TALs could be read from Jacob J. Akol's interview with Dr A Lokuji (Gurtong Peace Project, March 2008) that:

... First and foremost, they [TALs] are the only institution many of us in traditional localities know. The district commissioner and any government official from the towns are visitors and often have to be introduced even to the way the communities they are visiting think. In spite of the fifty years of independence, the governance we inherited from colonialists has not penetrated our cultures and still remains strange to the vast majority of our peoples. I believe that the majority members of our rural household could never talk to a government official without consent from their community leaders…

More findings on TAL roles and status are available in works on South Sudan and Africa by Wassara (2008), Kuol (2008) and many more South Sudanese and others. These studies support TALs' own perception and justify the significance of the proposed TAL consultative forums in Diagrams 3 and 5 above. King Wilson Hassan Peni, King of Zandeland, Western Equatoria state, once interviewed by Jacob Akol of the Gurtong Peace Project (March 2008), stated that: 'It [the consultative forum] is very important because it will bring unity to Southern Sudan'.

King Wilson added:

…During the conference in 2004, he [Dr John Garang] mentioned that it would be very important for the chiefs to meet every year at all area administrative levels. When chiefs are gathered, they will discuss issues that are affecting them and settle issues that can bring conflict among the people…

King Wilson concluded that:

...There are always cases to judge. When there is a conflict between individuals or communities, it is our duty to bring peace and reconciliation. We [the chiefs] also support the government in mobilizing the community to construct feeder roads, to construct health centres and mobilize children to go to school. Chiefs have a lot to do. King Wilson posed an important question: But if, like the moment, we [the chiefs] are not involved in policymaking, who will implement that policy? The government cannot just sit and make policy without involving the chiefs. It is the chiefs who can implement all government policies involving the people...

As highlighted by King Wilson, Diagrams 3 and 5 above explain the necessary national and state consultative forums referred to as the House of the Peoples at national and state levels respectively.

Envisioned five constituent units in public administration

The overall goal of this chapter is to enable all stakeholders and community members to appreciate and, in a timely manner, to implement constitutional and statutory mandates pertaining to the recognition of the status and roles of COTALs at all levels of governments in South Sudan. The intention is to maximise the potential of rural citizens and their community-based organisations, throughout multinational and multicultural South Sudan, to achieve the goals of the government agenda of *Taking Towns to Rural Areas* and promoting unity in diversity.

The government has made moves to prioritise the implementation of decentralisation. This move is in response to expressed demands for decentralisation exhibited countrywide. Though differing in terms of mechanisms and the number of proposed additional administrative states, the move has been explicitly expressed within and amongst a sizeable number of political parties in the country. Decentralisation was a popular demand by the All Tribes Conference in February 2015 in Juba. On 2 October 2015, President Kiir announced Establishment Order Number 36/2015 for the creation of the 28 states in the decentralised governance system in the Republic of South Sudan. The establishment order clearly stated that creating 28 states is with a goal of implementing the constitutional vision of decentralisation in the political, cultural, social and economic sectors. The order was reinforced by an amendment to article 162 of the SSTC 2011, widening the powers of the executive to create more states, which was passed by the Legislative Assembly. On 24 December 2015 President Kiir appointed governors to the 28 new states in accordance with provisions of EO/36/2015.

In fulfilment of the supremacy of rule of law, the legal parameters for recognition of the TALs and their communities are founded on the constitution and LGA 2009. In that, the following provisions are explicitly mandated in SSTC 2011. Article 165(6)(i) states: 'The objects of local government shall be to: (i) acknowledge and incorporate the role of Traditional Authority and customary law in the local government system'. Article 166(1) states: 'The institution, status and role of Traditional Authority, according to customary law, are recognised under this Constitution'. Article 169(1) states: 'The people of South Sudan own all land in South Sudan and that the government in accordance with the provisions of the Constitution and the law shall regulate land usage'.

These provisions are legally mandated under LGA 2009. Section 19(2) of LGA 2009 provides that the traditional leaders shall represent their people in the County Legislative Council as determined by this Act and regulations there under'. Section 19(3) mandates that the *boma* shall be the main domain of the traditional authority where traditional leaders perform their administrative and customary functions. Section 107 recognises the community, composed of clans, families and neighbourhoods, having the right to organise its governance under customary laws. In conformity to the use of the term 'traditional authority', section 112 describes them as semi-autonomous authorities. The traditional authority is divided in two categories: kingdom and chieftainship (with subchiefs and headmen). Kingdoms have a particular status, namely 'self-existing traditional systems' (section 113(2)), whereas chiefs are 'autonomous' and chosen by the people-community in a TCFS (section 114). In rural South Sudan, it is not only the people who determine the boundaries of the chieftainships, but this is also governed by statutory law (section 114(3)). These provisions justify the need to adopt five constituent units in South Sudan as suggested under Model 2 below.

In South Sudan, there are two basic principles that guide implementation of the laws and the political will. One is the principle of diversity of traditions as mandated by article 33 and 36(4) of SSTC 2001. The second is subsidiarity: (i) diversity of traditions and customs – the importance of this principle derives from the constitutional provision that one of the sources of law in South Sudan is the customs and traditions of the people(s) of South Sudan as explicitly provided under articles 5(c) and 5(d) of the SSTC 2011 on customs and traditions of the peoples and the will of the peoples respectively. Inherent in this principle is the concept of respect for diverse customs/traditions and inclusivity, that is, respecting the traditional self-government of each of the peoples and their right to life, namely to live in peaceful coexistence without one dominating the other, and (ii) subsidiarity – the term has constitutional status in the SSTC 2011 – mandates national government to promote to promote devolving powers to the peoples so that they can direct their own affairs (art. 168(1)). LGA 2009 explicitly defines subsidiarity as delegating decisions and functions to the lowest competent level of government (section 13(1)), which, as shown above, is the *boma.*

The mandated and indispensable support for the status and roles of TALs could not be overemphasised if it is stated that it has been recognised as pivotal in all spheres and aspects leading to enhancing peaceful coexistence, remorsefulness and justice in multinational and multicultural South Sudan. Also various research findings and recommendations and opinion polls conducted to date in South Sudan concur with a view of the centrality of the roles of TALs in building inclusive justice and democracy in a modern state. At the same time, the TALs have not been satisfactorily institutionalised as required under constitutional and statutory provisions and principles so that they can fulfil their duties to be the foundation for peaceful democratic coexistence in a multicultural South Sudan.

Institute LGB as an authority under MoFA to devolve Federal Powers

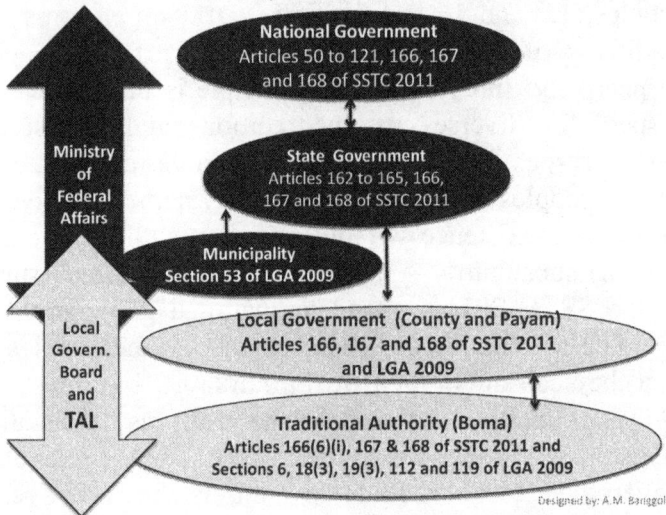

Diagram 7: Model 2 – Role of the Local Government Board as an authority within the Ministry of Federal Affairs

Diagram 7 depicts the LGB as an authority within the Ministry of Federal Affairs (MoFA). Its role is to connect with the MoFA at national and state levels, on the one hand, and with the local government in county and *payam* on the other. The purpose is to tell the reader that *boma* should be an exclusive domain of an elected or a selected traditional authority as mandated by section 19(3) of Local Government Act 2009 and articles 166, 167 and 168 of SSTC 2011.

The timely institutionalisation of the mandated TAL institutions at all levels of government in South Sudan is recommended. They could serve as pragmatic mechanisms and instruments that are able to augment the envisioned unity in diversity in South Sudan. Lessons learnt from the study tour concur with these views on managing diversity and should be further explored. The perception of a House of Federation in the Federal Republic of Ethiopia enhanced mutuality and consultative forums amongst the 74 nationalities leading to the timely harmony and mutuality. This is a successful model that is being adapted as the House of Peoples in this proposed framework for South Sudan. Also, in their report: *The principles of federalism* (Koller et al. 2012: 17–18), experts on the celebrated and successful cantons and communes of Swiss federalism warned that:

> ...Efforts to deny or suppress multiple identities within a diverse society have almost invariably led to contentions, secessions or civil wars. An essential element therefore in federation involving a diverse society has been the acceptance of the value of diversity and of possibility of multiple loyalties expressed through the established constituent units of government with genuine autonomous self-rule over those matters most important to their

distinct identity. Equally important has been the recognition of the benefits within a diverse society to be derived from shared purpose and objectives providing the basis for the parallel processes of shared rules...

Consistently with the same cognizance that praises mutual recognition of the largest communal federalism, the Bengali poet and winner of the Nobel Prize in Literature Rabindranath Tagore (1861–1941), in his poem 'Unity in Diversity' (1915), says

We are all the more one, because we are many,
For we have made ample room for love in the
gap where we are sundered.
Our unlikeness reveals its breadth of beauty
radiant with one common life
like mountain peaks in the morning sun.

In other words, although we are separated by our cultures and norms, love emerges precisely in this separation. We share one life and all strive for freedom, peace and prosperity, and it is in our differences that our beauty is born. We are united in our diversity.

Warning against hegemony and exclusion, in South Sudan, Jacob Akol once characterised the essence of social disharmony that has bedevilled African countries as follows:

...While they remained suspended and relatively peaceful in their corner of the net through the colonial period – contained by a better organised and superior power – the lifting of the colonial net at independence left most African nations ill-prepared for a constitution that should have endorsed the reality that the so-called 'African tribes' should have been better redefined in the constitutions in more dignified terms such as 'nationalities' and accepting that all those with a living language have cultural values. Once this notion is accepted, it follows that cultural values are equal, no matter how large or small an ethnic community. This notion is inclusive and does not in any way discriminate anyone but communicates the noble notion of 'unity in diversity'. It did not happen that way in most cases in Africa. [The mistake that happened with independence is that] the larger communities stepped into the colonial shoes by taking advantage of their greater numbers in an attempt to control and govern over the colonial geographical boundaries, assuming that the smaller communities would be all 'patriotic' and would understand the good intentions of those in power. It seemed to work for a while following the euphoria of having got rid of what was commonly seen as an alien power over the common pool; but it soon fell apart due to either greed for wealth or power or both by elites of the larger communities who found themselves in power. The result has been coups and counter-coups, civil wars, famine and general instability throughout much of Africa. These are sad facts about Africa, which those with blinkers on and eyes focused on a blanket and wishful constitution, will not entertain...

The wisdom in South Sudan should be to avoid repeating the same marginalisation against which South Sudan nationalities collaborated to wage armed struggle. This injustice was rejected by the overwhelming vote against it in 2001. The level of success and sustainable social coherence and unity in diversity in South Sudan should be anchored on the level of recognition of TCFSs and their TAL institutions in crafting the envisioned permanent constitution in South Sudan. This could allow mutuality and routinised consultative forums to address disputes and build mutual trust.

In support of unity in diversity and mutuality through consultative forums, Kwacakworo-Conradin Berner in Gurtong (2008) advised that in perception of cultural values

... [n]umbers do not count in the cultural question. If you have ten people with a culture and you have one person with a culture, they are all equal and need the same respect. If people respect each other's values it will lead to dialogue, will lead to understanding and will lead to unity. Problems will always be there, but when there is respect for values there will always be a way for dialogue to solve those problems. That is the value of forming these councils of traditional leaders as means of resolving conflicts...

This is established under articles 33 and 36(4) of SSTC 2011.

The ideal solution is to advance in explaining the essence of unity in diversity, suggesting togetherness for a common purpose without assimilation. Instead of allowing cultural diversity to fragment the society, the focus is to work for tolerance and mutual recognition. Unity in diversity dissuades against narrow-mindedness, while celebrating diversity in thoughts and norms through direct dialogue and allowing desired commonality of a common purpose to surface. Unity in diversity should be followed within a comprehension that different cultural identities enrich our South Sudanese empathic connectivity and interactions. It suggests love towards a South Sudanese mosaic of cultures and beautiful traits, where everyone collectively and emphatically identifies with commonality, camaraderie and companionship as comrades of one destiny. This can be sensed in the coat of arms of the Republic of South Sudan, representing unity in peace and harmony. Unity in diversity is love to oneself and others, as we would want others to love us, and celebrating our varied styles and manifestations. Unity in diversity denotes mutuality and collaborative interdependence where, in a culturally diverse society like multicultural South Sudan, our diversity should be regarded as richness in cultural values, such that the 72 nationalities of South Sudan in their discrete thousands of cultural identities can peacefully coexist. This means an egalitarian society where everyone is an entity and every culture counts and is mutually reliable and responsible for the happiness of all by all.

Reflections on the envisioned twining

In the Republic of South Sudan, a quick look into historical records indicates that with the onset of colonisation in the 19th century of Old Sudan and now South Sudan, the colonisers were confronted with armed resistance led by TALs. The resistance was in the form of collaboration or was spontaneously carried out single-handedly by communes, as TCFSs. In historical records TCFSs are popularly known as chiefdoms or kingdoms. Contrary to the mistaken view that the British colonisers established TALs, the TALs in fact existed before colonisation. Above all the TAL institutions maintain relevance in the modern political nation-state. In reality, the failure to fully subjugate TALs or force them to capitulate, surrender and cede their powers led the British colonial administration at later stages to incorporate the roles of TALs as subordinate agents. The obvious purpose was that TALs would advance community labour mobilisation, tax collection, control of order and continue their restorative justice through community arbitration, popularly referred to as customary laws. However, the British colonial administration limited their investment and incorporation of TAL capacities to promote internal and external community border tranquillity, peace dialogue, mutuality and peaceful coexistence in sharing common natural resources. TALs were denied involvement in issues of good governance that should have allowed communities to become involved in decisions that influence rural communities. It is noted that there is some spillover of these attitudes of bad governance.

The evolutionary process of the importance of TALs could be noted in the history of liberation in South Sudan. By 12–13 June 1947 a paradigm shift had occurred, in which TALs became the major discussant on the political future of the then Southern Sudan region. Since 1956, the role of TALs has been incorporated in local government, but with a similar perception of top-down colonial administration that excluded the same TAL system of governance. TAL institutions were incorporated as lesser and subsidiary administrative constituent units. The resultant negative impact is that TALs were mistakenly perceived and treated as the staff of local administrators to implement government orders. The element of two-way communication was not a factor in the process of public administration.

In the history of armed and political liberation in South Sudan 1955–2005, the period 1983–2004 saw the demonstrated importance of the role of TAL institutions. During these difficult years, the then public administration by Khartoum collapsed. TAL institutions were recognised as the only viable public administration throughout rural South Sudan, controlled by the SPLA. TAL institutions became central in leading the mobilisation of human and material resources in support of armed struggle while fully filling the gap in public administration. By 2003, the SPLM's vision of *Taking Towns to Rural Peoples*, which was built on the success story of TAL institutions, evolved with a view to incorporate the roles and status of TALs. The success influenced the framers of SPLM ideological perception and legislation. There are now explicit constitutional and legal provisions and mandates on the socio-polity, economy and inclusive, just and good governance of South Sudan with huge reference to TAL institutions. During the 2008 census, the 2010 elections and the 2011 referendum, the role of TALs was pivotal in mobilisation and peaceful process within their communities. The role of TAL institutions was crowned with the credible, peaceful, near-unanimous result of 98.83% in support of the secession of South Sudan and the founding of the Republic of South Sudan on 9 July 2011.

Various studies and findings, recommendations and opinion polls conducted to date in South Sudan concur with a view of the centrality of the roles of TAL institutions in building a modern nation-state. This should be consummated in the form of twining of the political nation-state on the one hand with the TCFSs led by TALs on the other. The goal of such a twining is to ensure inclusive, just and good governance in multinational and multicultural South Sudan. Though not satisfactorily institutionalised, there are favourable views cognizant of the indispensable and necessary crosscutting roles of TALs and their institutions. These, if explored in a timely fashion, could effectively and efficiently enhance the mutual promotion of peaceful coexistence and remorsefulness amongst and within a multinational and multicultural South Sudan united in diversity.

The proposed House of the Peoples (Diagram 3 and Diagram 5 above) is envisaged as annual or biannual meetings to bring the existing bicameral house of National Assembly and Council of States on the one hand and the national COTAL on the other to form a consultative House of the Peoples for national or state-level dialogue for wider ownership and inclusive collaborative decision-making processes and actions.

Considering the legal provisions, it is logical to propose that the *boma* administration as mandated by sections 6 and 19(3) of LGA 2009 is recognised as an autonomous constituent unit from the local government. *Boma* should be considered the third layer and a domain of the TAL institutions in the envisioned twining. This could serve as a collaborative social and political contract between the political nation-state (nation, state, county and *payam*) and the history-long societal nation-state of TCFSs and TAL systems of customary public administration. The *boma* constituent units being the TCFSs should be recognised as the government layers closer to the rural peoples throughout South Sudan. It is assumed that each of the newly established administrative states will be mandated by amended article 162(1) of SSTC 2011 and the defunct state constitutions will be repealed in accordance to SSTC 2011 and EO36/2015.

Program outline of COTAL development and empowerment

Model 1, above, depicts that each of the several administrative states out of each of the three geopolitical greater regions of South Sudan is in content made up of a number of TCFSs of governance. Considering its legal mandate under section 19(3) of LGA 2009, a TCFS is institutionally identified as a *boma* administration. The TCFS is represented by model 2, above, depicting the mandated *boma* administrative unity, the TCFS, under TALs. In that, the TCFS, the *boma* administrative constituent unit, should be recognised as the governance system closer to the rural people(s) in the country. It supports a view suggesting five administrative constituent units. The TCFS led by TALs is recognised

157

as the unit block that should be empowered by the nation-state and the development actors, as the corner stone in building unity in diversity amongst 72 nationalities in multicultural and multinational South Sudan. TALs, through TCFSs, could enhance the achievement of *Taking Towns to Rural Peoples in South Sudan*. In that, the mandated COTALs could serve as clusters at *payam*, county, state and national levels. The national gathering is depicted in Diagrams 3 and 5 as the House of the Peoples at national and state level.

Earlier on, the indispensable roles of TALs was attested during the British Administration and proved significant through postcolonial Old Sudan, during the 1983–2004 armed struggle, the implementation of a peace agreement, and the referendum, suggesting their relevance now and in the foreseeable future. Research and opinion polls confirm their popular support. TALs proved to be connectors between the political nation-state and development partners with programs to serve communities in rural South Sudan. Every single internal and cross-cultural peace program highlights the necessity of TALs to enhance implementation and to cement peaceful coexistence and reconciliation.

Neglecting TAL institutions and TCFSs is not only unconstitutional, but could be a lost opportunity. If effectively supported, TAL clusters, COTALs and Houses of the Peoples could enhance direct dialogue, leading to consensus on mutual recognition and confidence building amongst conferee TALs and their communities. The process could serve as a platform for launching interventions and collaborative learning about needed local and national security and mutuality to amicably create win–win coexistence amongst the mobile cattle herders and the settler farmers. It could be an annual or biannual forum to test the level of cooperation and a medium to promote accountability within and amongst the TALs and TCFSs on the mutual benefit from the shared natural resources. These forums could allow mechanisms of declaration of cooperation and connectedness amongst the TALs. Youth, women and cultural groups could be involved to allow nearness and fraternity, which could be further enhanced by social media and phone contacts.

The following suggests a framework that could be used in designing COTAL development and empowerment at local, state and national levels in the Republic of South Sudan.

Program goals

TALs help contribute to achieving Sustainable Development Goal #16 (peace, justice and strong institutions), which is dedicated to the promotion of peaceful and inclusive societies for sustainable development, the provision of access to justice for all and building effective, accountable institutions at all levels.

With regard to the principle of subsidiarity, the program shall allow full implementation of section 19(3) of LGA 2009, which mandates *boma* to be the main domain of TALs to perform their administrative and customary roles. In that, section 107 recognises that the community, composed of clans, families and neighbourhoods, has the right to organise its governance under customary laws. Section 8(1) stipulates that 'The

Local Government Authority shall be **derived** from the people and shall be exercised in accordance with the peoples' will as prescribed in this Act and any other applicable laws in the country' [my emphasis].

Concerning adherence to constitutional articles, article 166(6)(c) of SSTC 2011 (rev. 2013) states that 'all levels of government shall encourage the involvement of community based organizations in the matters of local government and promote dialogue amongst them on matters of local interest'.

With strict regard to the principle of subsidiarity, article 168(2) of SSTC 2011 (rev. 2013) mandates that '[l]legislation at the national and state levels shall provide for the establishment, composition, functions and duties of councils for Traditional Authority leaders', this being done, however, with regard to the constitutional provisions of article 48 that the national government is only to coordinate and provide 'norms', so that the link to the local government is only through the state.

With strict regard to the principle of subsidiarity, article 37(2)(d) of SSTC 2011 (rev. 2013) mandates that all levels of government 'shall promote private initiative and self-reliance and take all necessary steps to involve the people in the formulation and implementation of development plans and programs that affect them and enhance as well their right to equal opportunities in development'.

Program inputs

- Professional services

- Transport, travel and accommodation of participants and resource persons
- Funding of 3- to 5-day conferences
- Follow-up, capacity-building fund to further consult with and train TALs, representatives of their communities, and their support staff.

Program activities

PASS consultants are to engage a resource person from the Botswana Ministry of Local Government and Traditional Authority to embark on a study and the completion of a manual for TALs to be involved in public administration in the targeted state in the Republic of South Sudan.

PASS consultants are to engage an identified international consultant to explore the lessons learnt and to fashion a dialogue on how to implement the State COTAL Act and LGA 2009 in consultation with TALs and their communities with emphasis on subsidiarity at the sub-state levels. New research surveys need to determine the extent of accountability of TALs to their communities.

PASS consultants in collaboration with the targeted state government are to organise a 5-day conference with TALs, communities and stakeholders to explain the program and to seek participants' input.

PASS consultants need funds to engage an expert from the Botswana Ministry of Local Government and Traditional Authority to help design the program that could enhance viability, sustainability, involvement and recognition of the status and roles of TALs.

Funds are needed to ensure continuous engagement by PASS consultants and resource personnel to support the targeted state legislature, the executive and the civil society on what is appropriate legislation, and how to design relevant policies and programs to develop and empower COTALs in the states of South Sudan.

Potential funding from interested parties needs to be sought to engage professional services for developing iSDG modelling expertise adapted to the targeted state in particular, which could enable a process of dialogue and consensus on peace and development issues. The adapted iSDG model is expected to come up with options to meet the goals of *Taking Towns to Rural Peoples*.

Program outputs

- Embark on a study and completion of a TAL Manual on Public Administration to fulfil mandate of articles 166(6)(c), 167, 168 and 169(3) of SSTC 2011, COTAL Act in the targeted state of South Sudan and section 19(3) of LGA 2009.
- Embark on a study and dialogue on ways and means to allow the COTAL Development and Empowerment Program in the targeted state to be widely owned by communities and their TALs, the targeted state government and the stakeholders.
- State COTALs will be formed on the basis of the principle of subsidiarity and TAL status and roles are recognised at all levels in the targeted state constitution and adapted State COTAL Act.
- The *boma* level is recognised as a sustainable and viable domain under TALs in *Taking Towns to Rural*

Peoples in targeted states of South Sudan by bringing the decision-making process to the communities.

- *Boma* administration is recognised as viable and could enhance the roles of citizens and their community-based organisations and TALs to take responsibility for economic and cultural programs leading to inclusive, just, democratic and good governance.

Program outcome

- Effective and efficient implementation of constitutional and legal mandates alongside the political will to empower TALs and rural communities to be involved in decisions on all issues that influence their livelihoods and socioeconomic progress and enhance their corruption-free, democratic self-governance.
- TALs through state COTALs shall engage in regular consultative forums to enhance collective networking, emphatic listening and mutual respect in discourse, collaborative learning, deep thinking and strategic navigations.
- The citizens, community-based organisations, TALs and their communities and State COTALs set an example nationally for inclusive, just and good governance.

Program indicators

- Report on the conference
- Number of participants

- Framework for a manual on the roles of TAL institutions in public administration in the beneficiary state

- Recommendations of a consultative forum amongst the stakeholders in the state on the enforcement of a State COTAL Act

- Findings and recommendations by experts on local government

- Recommendations by experts from the Botswana Ministry of Local Government and Traditional Affairs on the viability and sustainability of the *boma* governance unit under TALs

- Level of awareness of TALs and stakeholders in a beneficiary state concerning actual and potential allocation of funding to the rural economy to promote self-reliance and wealth creation

- Periodic reports by PASS consultants.

Program impact

At a beneficiary state level, the program could help (a) improve inclusive, just and good governance with increased involvement, incorporation and recognition of the status and roles of TALs on matters that influence socio-polity, economic and cultural aspects in the targeted state; (b) reduce rural–urban migration; and (c) encourage rural youth to engage in self-employment in agriculture, livestock raising and marketing.

At the national level, PASS consultants can enthuse decision-makers to see the value of a National Council of Traditional Leaders under article 168(1) and (2) of the SSTC 2011 and sections 118 and 120 of the LAG and offer intensive consultation with the communities of the TALS about their authority and terms of formation.

At a targeted state level, impact of the program shall include ability to institutionalise article 166(6)(c) on encouragement of communities and community-based institutions to good governance so that TALs and COTALs could meet periodically with the government to seek accountability on the Community Development Fund, The Logoseed Program and other programs that target the rural communities.

Program performance measurement or monitoring plan

PASS consultants have learnt many lessons through engaging in advocacy for the establishment of COTALs in South Sudan since 2006 and through participation in the familiarisation tour by South Sudanese TALs to Botswana, Ghana and South Africa in January 2013. The founder and chief researcher of the PASS consultants, who researched on the roles of TALs in *Taking Towns to Rural Peoples in South Sudan*, shall lead the PASS consultant team. PASS consultants, subject to availability of resources, shall engage in supervisory roles that shall ensure continuous monitoring and evaluation, as well as empowering TALs to advocate for policies and mechanisms through which *boma* and its inhabitant citizens themselves could widely own and interactively participate in design monitoring and evaluation procedures. PASS consultants could be supported to extend the lessons learnt from the familiarisation tour to Ghana, South Africa and Botswana. Resource persons could be invited to advise on the necessary institutional framework and organisational culture that could allow viability and sustainability of *boma* administrative units under TALs.

APPENDICES

TAKING TOWNS TO RURAL PEOPLES
The Roles of Traditional Authority Leaders
Republic of South Sudan

Closed-ended Questionnaire

Please respond to the following closed-ended questions.

1. Sex:
   Male: _____   Female: _____

2. Title: _____

3. Are you aware of the provisions of SSTC 2011 and Local Government Act 2009 on the status, roles and functions of Traditional Authority Leaders (TALs) and Councils of Traditional Authority Leaders (COTALs) at National, State and Local Government (County, Payam and Boma) levels?

   | Y | | N |

4. Do you agree that TAL and their related COTAL at national, state and local government levels have complementary roles to all levels of executive and legislature in accordance with Article 166(6)(c): *'...encourage the involvement of communities and community based organizations in the matters of local government in order to promote dialogue among them on matters of local interest...',* Article

167

169(3) '...*the National Government shall promote and encourage the participation of the people in the formulation of its development policies and programs...*', read together with Section 19(1) '...*the administration aspects of TAL institutions and systems shall be incorporated in the three tiers of the Local Government...*' and 19(2) '...*TAL shall be the main domain of Traditional Authority where traditional leaders perform their administrative and customary functions...*'?

Y	N

5. Do you agree that there is a need to add a provision on competence of National Legislative Assembly after Article 55(3)(d) '...*to consult with National COTAL in compliance with Article 168(2) and 169(3) of SSTC 2011...*'?

Y	N

6. Do you agree that there is a need to add a provision on Council of States after article 60(3)(b) so that any bill passed by National Legislative Assembly that affects the status, roles and functions of TAL shall be referred to National COTAL for scrutiny in accordance with provisions on roles of Traditional Authority that Legislature at the National level shall provide for the establishment, composition, functions and duties of National COTAL?

Y	N

7. Do you agree that there is a need to add a provision on Functions of the President after Article 101(g) to be: '...*to convene, summon, adjourn or prorogue the National COTAL in consultation with Chairman of National COTAL in accordance Article 168(2) of SSTC2011...*'?

Y		N

8. Do you agree that there is a need to add a provision on Functions of Council of Ministers after 110(h) to read: '...*to provide reports upon request by the National COTAL in accordance with Article 168(2) of SSTC 2011...*'?

Y		N

9. Do you agree that there is a need to add a provision on Functions of Council of Ministers after 169(5) to read: '...*to consult National COTAL on sharing and allocation of resources and national wealth before presenting to National Legislature accordance with Articles 166, 167 and 168(2) of SSTC 2011...*'?

Y		N

10. Do you agree that there is a need to add a provision on primary responsibilities of the Local Government Council to ensure that the Council roles are compliance with a need to consult with County level COTAL in accordance with sections 6(3) of Local Government working with levels closest to the Peoples?

Y		N

11. Do you agree that there is a need to add a provision on Powers and Functions of the Executive Council after Section 47(f) to read: '...*to report to County COTAL in accordance with Section 19 of Local Government Act 2009 and Article 168(2) of SSTC 2011...*'?

Y	N

12. Do you agree that there is a need to add a provision on Powers and Functions of the County Commissioner after Section 52 (d) to read: '...*to execute on policies and traditional customary laws passed by County COTAL...*' and according to Section 52 (f) '...*to initiates traditional covenant and amends to County COTAL and assents and signs them into traditional customary laws...*' and according to Section 52 (g) '... *to summons and adjourns or prorogues the County COTAL in consultation with the Chairman of County COTAL...*'?

Y	N

13. Do you agree that there is a need to add a provision on Powers and Functions of the Mayor after Article 57(d) '...*Traditional Customary Laws passed by COTAL in accordance to Sections 19 of Local Government Act 2009 in accordance with Articles 166, 167 and 168 of SSTC 2011...*'?

Y	N

14. Do you agree that there is a need to add a provision on Powers and Functions of County Executive Director after Article 65(e), which supervises the administration of COTAL?

Y		N

15. Do you agree that there is a need to add a provision on Powers and Functions of Town Clerk after Article 65(d) to implement decisions and programs of COTAL?

Y		N

16. Do you agree that there is a need to add a provision on Powers and Functions of Local Government Administrator to be incorporated under Article 66?

Y		N

17. Do you agree that there is a need to add a provision on Powers and Functions of Local Officer under Section 67?

Y		N

18. Do you agree that there is a need to add a provision on Powers and Functions of Seconded Staff under Section 70?

Y		N

19. Do you agree that there is a need to add a provision on implementation of the COTAL to be incorporated under article 72?

Y		N

20. Do you agree that there is a need to add a provision on competence of Fiscal and Financial Allocation and Monitoring Commission to be able to engage National, State and County COTAL to fulfill its mandate on article 181 (1) and (2) of SSTC 2011?

Y		N

21. Could the establishment, composition, functions and duties of TAL and their COTAL enhance the realization of 'Taking Towns to Rural Areas'?

Y		N

This marks the end of our interview. Do you have any questions for me? Thanks for your participating in this study.

Appendix 2: Open-ended study questionnaire
TAKING TOWNS TO RURAL PEOPLES
The Roles of Traditional Authority Leaders in the
Republic of South Sudan

Open-ended Study Questionnaire
Focused Group Discussion

Please respond to the following closed- and open-ended questions.

1. Are you aware of the provisions of SSTC 2011 and Local Government Act 2009 on status, roles and functions of Traditional Authority Leaders (TAL) and Council of Traditional Authority Leaders (COTAL) at National, State and Local Government (County, Payam and Boma) levels?

Y		N

If no, why?

2. Do you agree that TAL and their related COTAL at national, state and local government levels have complementary roles to all levels of executive and legislature in accordance with Article 166(6)(c): *'...encourage the involvement of communities and community based organizations in the matters of local government in order to promote dialogue*

among them on matters of local interest...'. Article
169(3) *'...the National Government shall promote
and encourage the participation of the people in the
formulation of its development policies and
programs...'* read together with Section 19(1) *'...the
administration aspects of TAL institutions and
systems shall be incorporated in the three tiers of the
Local Government...'* and 19(2) *'...TAL shall be the
main domain of Traditional Authority where
traditional leaders perform their administrative and
customary functions...'*?

Y		N

If yes/no, why?

3. Do you agree that there is a need to add a provision
   on competence of National Legislative Assembly
   after Article 55(3)(d) *'...to consult with National
   COTAL in compliance with Article 168(2) and
   169(3) of SSTC 2011...'*?

Y		N

If yes/no, why?

4. Do you agree that there is a need to add a provision
   on Council of States after article 60(3)(b) so that any
   bill passed by National Legislative Assembly that
   affects the status, roles and functions of TAL shall be

referred to National COTAL for scrutiny in
compliance with provisions on roles of Traditional
Authority that Legislature at the National level shall
provide for the establishment, composition, functions
and duties of National COTAL?

Y	N

If yes/no, why?

5. Do you agree that there is a need to add a provision
on Functions of the President after Article 101(g) to
be: '...*to convene, summon, adjourn or prorogue the
National COTAL in consultation with Chairman of
National COTAL in accordance Article 168(2) of
SSTC 2011...*'?

Y	N

If yes/no, why?

6. Do you agree that there is a need to add a provision
on Functions of Council of Ministers after 110(h) to
read: '...*to provide reports upon request by the
National COTAL in accordance with Article 168(2)
of SSTC 2011...*'?

Y	N

If yes/no, why?

7. Do you agree that there is a need to add a provision on Functions of Council of Ministers after 169(5) to read: '...*to consult National COTAL on sharing and allocation of resources and national wealth before presenting to National Legislature accordance with Articles 166, 167 and 168(2) of SSTC 2011...*'?

Y	N

If yes/no, why?

8. Do you agree that there is a need to add a provision on primary responsibilities of the Local Government Council to read: '...*to ensure that the Council roles are compliance with a need to consult with County level COTAL in accordance with sections 6(3) of Local Government working with levels closest to the People...*'?

Y	N

If yes/no, why?

9. Do you agree that there is a need to add a provision on Powers and Functions of the Executive Council after Section 47(f) to read: '...*to report to County COTAL in accordance with Section 19 of Local Government Act 2009 and Article 168(2) of SSTC 2011...*'?

Y	N

If yes/no, why?

10. Do you agree that there is a need to add a provision on Powers and Functions of the County Commissioner after Section 52 (d) to read: *'...to execute on policies and traditional customary laws passed by County COTAL...'* and in compliance with Section 52 (f) to read: *'...initiates traditional covenant and amends to County COTAL and assents and signs them into traditional customary laws...'* and together with Section 52 (g) to read: *'...summons and adjourns or prorogues the County COTAL in consultation with the Chairman of County COTAL...'*?

Y		N

If yes/no, why?

11. Do you agree that there is a need to add a provision on Powers and Functions of the Mayor after Article 57(d) to read *'...Traditional Customary Laws passed by COTAL in accordance to Sections 19 of Local Government Act 2009 in accordance with Articles 166, 167 and 168 of SSTC 2011...'*?

Y		N

If yes/no, why?

12. Do you agree that there is a need to add a provision on Powers and Functions of County Executive Director after Article 65(e) to read: '...*which supervises the administration of COTAL*'?

Y	N

If yes/no, why?

13. Do you agree that there is a need to add a provision on Powers and Functions of Town Clerk after Article 65(d) to read: '...*to implement decisions and programs of COTAL...*'?

Y	N

If yes/no, why?

14. Do you agree that there is a need to add a provision on Powers and Functions of Local Government Administrator to be incorporated under Section 66?

Y	N

If yes/no, why?

15. Do you agree that there is a need to add a provision on Powers and Functions of Local Officer under Section 67?

Y	N

If yes/no, why?

16. Do you agree that there is a need to add a provision on Powers and Functions of Seconded Staff under Section 70?

Y		N

If yes/no, why?

17. Do you agree that there is a need to add a provision on implementation of the COTAL to be incorporated under article 72?

Y		N

If yes/no, why?

18. Do you agree that there is a need to add a provision on competence of Fiscal and Financial Allocation and Monitoring Commission to be able to engage National, State and County COTAL to fulfill its mandate on article 181 (1) and (2) of SSTC 2011?

Y		N

If yes/no, why?

19. Could the establishment, composition, functions and duties of TAL and their COTAL to enhance the realization of 'Taking Towns to Rural Peoples' as a program?

Y		N

If yes/no, why?

20. What do you think are the
    a. opportunities,
    b. challenges, and
    c. prospectives
    of creating a Consultative Forum at each of the following:
    - (i) National Consultative Forum (National Legislature and National COTAL)
    - (ii) State Consultative Forum (State Legislature and State COTAL)
    - (iii) County Consultative Forum (County Legislative Assembly and County COTAL)?

    What strategies do you suggest to mitigate these challenges?

This marks the end of our interview. Do you have any questions for me? Thanks for your participating in this study.

Appendix 3: COTAL-related recommendations

Recommendations arising out of the study and familiarisation tour of South Sudanese traditional leaders and government officials to South Africa, Botswana and Ghana, 13–31 January 2013

Following the above tour, South Sudanese Traditional Leaders and Government officials to South Africa, Botswana and Ghana, a scheduled debriefing session was held by all participants of the tour at the Jacaranda Hotel, Nairobi/ Kenya on 31 January 2013. The following are the recommendations that were made at the meeting:

1. A speedy implementation to the Local Government Act 2009 was suggested.
2. There is a need to establish oversight ministries, which will, amongst other functions, cater for the institution of traditional leadership structures.
3. The meeting was of the view that there should be very clear terms of reference articulated by the Government of South Sudan (GoSS) for all levels and sub-structures of COTALs.
4. Efforts should be made to train chiefs regarding GoSS expectation, the exact structure and linkages between Government and COTALs.
5. It was recommended that efforts should be directed towards the completion of the setting up of COTALs, as soon as possible.
6. Consideration needs to be given to the scheduling of the first conference for all chiefs to introduce to them

the ideas and practice of COTALs. The feature could take place on a more rigorous state basis.

7. Create gender-sensitivity and gender-mainstreaming to be applied to all substructures and institutions related to the COTAL process.
8. Attention should be given to building the capacities of traditional leaders.
9. Traditional leaders should avoid political involvement. If a traditional leader chooses active political involvement, he or she should step down.
10. Personal enrichment by traditional leaders should be strictly avoided.
11. Efforts should be made towards cooperation between COTALs.

Appendix 4: Powers and functions of Ntlo ya Dikagosi in Republic of Botswana

The functions of Ntlo ya Dikagosi

The roles of Ntlo ya Dikagosi are quite different from that of the National Assembly. The functions of Ntlo ya Dikagosi as specified under the provision of section 85 of the Constitution of Botswana are rather informed by its conditional position as an advisory body with no legislative powers. Ntlo ya Dikagosi renders its advice on traditional customary and any other matters referred to it by the government or the National Assembly. Ntlo ya Dikagosi is entailed to submit its resolution to the National Assembly after consideration of any bill referred to it.

The clerk of the National Assembly, to accomplish its advisory mandate, shall forthwith lay the resolution that has been submitted to the National Assembly, before the Assembly. The constitution of Botswana permits Ntlo ya Dikagosi to exercise the following powers and functions.

1. *Consideration of bill:* the primary function of Ntlo ya Dikagosi is to consider any copy of a bill referred to it by the National Assembly under provisions of section 88 (2) of the Constitution of the Republic of Botswana. These are bills affecting tribal property, tribal organisation customary laws or the customary courts. Section 88(2) says:

- The National Assembly shall not proceed upon any Bill (including any amendment of a Bill) that, in the opinion of the person presiding, would if enacted alter any of the provisions of the constitution or affect

a) the designation, recognition, removal of powers of Chiefs, Sub-chiefs or Headmen;

the organization, power or administration of customary courts;

customary law or the ascertainment or recording of customary law; or

tribal organization or tribal property,

Unless

a. a copy of the Bill has been referred to Ntlo ya Dikagosi after it has been introduced in the National Assembly; and

a period of 30 days has elapsed from the date when the copy of the Bill was referred to Ntlo ya Dikagosi.

2. *Discuss matters of public interest:* The house is empowered to discuss any matter within the executive or legislative authority of Botswana which it considers desirable to take cognizance of in the interests of the tribes and tribal organizations it

represents and to make representations thereon to the president or to send messages thereon to the National Assembly.

3. *Provide advice to the Executive:* Ntlo ya Dikagosi may be consulted by any Minister in respect of any matter on which he or she desires to obtain the opinion of the house. Any Minister may consult Ntlo ya Dikagosi in respect of any matter on which he or she desires to obtain the opinion on Ntlo ya Dikagosi, and for that purpose the Minister or his or her representative may attend the proceedings of Ntlo ya Dikagosi.

Procedure on Bills in the Ntlo ya Dikagosi

When in terms of section 88(2) of the constitution a Bill has been referred to the House for its consideration, the Bill shall be considered according to the following procedure.

a) **First reading of the Bill**
   When the first reading of the bill is taken the Chairman shall move that the Bill be read for the first time, and a debate may then arise on the general merits and principles of the Bill.

b) **Second reading of the Bill**
   When the second reading of the bill is taken the Chairman shall read it the second time and then call

the number of each clause or of any groups of clauses in succession. On each clause or group of clauses being so called a debate may arise on the question covering the details of the clause or clauses called.

c) **Consideration of the House's resolution on the Bill**

When consideration of the House's resolution on a bill is taken any Member may bring a draft resolution on the Bill for the consideration of the House. The chairman shall move a draft in order until one is accepted as a basis for discussion. The house shall then go through the draft resolution paragraph by paragraph. When consideration of a draft resolution paragraph by paragraph is concluded and all motions relating to new paragraphs have been disposed of, the Chairman shall put the question that the resolution be the resolution of the House.

The secretary of Ntlo ya Dikagosi shall forward a copy of every such resolution, certified under his hand and the hand of the Chairman as a true copy to the Clerk of National assembly.

Attendance of Ministers in Ntlo ya Dikagosi

Any minister who is responsible for a Bill or a copy of which has been referred to Ntlo ya Dikagosi in terms of section 85(1) may attend the proceedings of the Ntlo ya

Dikagosi when the copy of the Bill is being considered. The following are other instances when a cabinet Minister may attend the proceedings:

a) The minister who has consulted the House on any matter may attend proceedings of the House relative to such matter.

b) Any minister who has arranged to make a statement to the House in pursuance of rule 20 may attend the proceedings of the House for the purpose of making such statement.

c) Any minister may be invited by the chairman to attend any other proceedings of the House.

A person attending the proceedings of the Ntlo ya Dikagosi by virtue of the above provisions shall be entitled to take part in those proceedings as if he or she were a Member of the House. But he or she shall not be entitled to vote in Ntlo ya Dikagosi.

Appendix 5: Officials of Ntlo ya Dikgosi in the Republic of Botswana

Office of Chairperson of Ntlo ya Dikgosi

The office of Chairperson of Ntlo ya Dikgosi is very important, for the orderly operation of Ntlo ya Dikgosi cannot carry on its proceedings without a Chairman. The office of Chairperson is established under rule 3 of the Rules of Procedure, which says there shall be a Chairman and Deputy Chairman of Ntlo ya Dikgosi.

Election of Chairperson

The Members of Ntlo ya Dikgosi elect the Chairperson to preside over its meetings as required by the constitution at the first meeting of the House in any given year or after a general election to the National Assembly or wherever the office is vacant. The members also elect the Deputy Chairperson to act as presiding officer during the unavoidable absence of the Chairperson and also to assist the Chairperson in carrying out his or her functions.

Ntlo ya Dikgosi elect the Chairperson and Deputy Chairperson following the procedure set out in the Second Schedule of the Rules of Procedure. It is provided for in the Rules of Procedure that the Secretary of Ntlo Ya Dikgosi shall preside over the election of the Chairperson and the person elected Chairperson will then preside over the election of the Deputy Chairperson.

The procedure commences with the presiding officer calling for any Member of the House to nominate any other Member for election as a Chairperson. The nomination must be seconded before the presiding officer calls upon the Member so nominated to declare whether he or she accepts candidature or not.

When all nominations have been received, the Secretary shall announce the names of all members who have been duly nominated and seconded and have accepted candidature, then the Presiding officer shall forthwith declare him/her to be elected as Chairperson. If more than one Member has been nominated and seconded and accepted candidature, a poll shall be taken.

The person so elected as Chairperson or Deputy Chairperson shall hold office until he or she resigns from such office by writing under his or her hand addressed to the Secretary, or ceases to be a Member of Ntlo ya Dikgosi or another person is elected as Chairman at an election held in pursuance of rule 3 of the Rules of Procedure.

Functions and Duties of the Chairperson
The Chairperson of Ntlo ya Dikgosi is expected to exercise the powers and functions outlined underneath:

1) *Chairing the House Proceedings:* The primary responsibility of the Chairperson of Ntlo ya Dikgosi is to preside over or chair the meetings of the House

and ensure that the decorum and order of the House is maintained. He or she ensures that the proceedings of the House are conducted according to the provisions of the Rules of Procedure. The Chairperson interprets and enforces the Rules of Procedure, responds to points of order as raised by Members, and makes rulings on questions of procedure when necessary.

2) *The Administrative Function:* The Chairperson is responsible through the office of the Secretary, for the administration of Ntlo ya Dikgosi and for ensuring that the staff provides Members of Ntlo ya Dikgosi with appropriate support service to facilitate their constitutional mandate.

3) *The Spokesperson of the House:* The chairman shall be the spokesperson of Ntlo Ya Dikagosi in the relation with other organs of government and with outside institutions and persons. The official communication or correspondence of Ntlo ya Dikgosi is signed or addressed to the Chairperson of Ntlo ya Dikgosi.

4) The Chairperson shall serve as a link between the house and the national bodies such as National AIDS Council, Rural Development council etc.

5) *Leads Delegations:* Represents Ntlo ya Dikgosi in International Conference, Seminars, SADC KHOTLA and workshops as leader of delegations. In such representation, the Chairperson shall be

accountable to Ntlo ya Dikgosi and to all its Members. He or she also welcomes and receives foreign delegation from similar Houses and other institution that visit the Ntlo ya Dikgosi.

The Chairperson is assisted in carrying out his duties by the Deputy Chairperson who is elected following the same procedure as that of electing the Chairperson.

Duties of the Deputy Chairperson of Ntlo ya Dikgosi

- Acting in the absence of the chairperson of the House.
- Assists the Chairperson to guide the House sittings.
- He/she may perform any duty as delegated by the Chairperson.
- Ensure effect and effect administration of the House.

Duties of Secretary of Ntlo ya Dikgosi

- The secretary is responsible for keeping minutes of all the proceedings of the House.
- The secretary is responsible for the production of an official report of all speeches made and all business transacted in the House.
- The secretary presides over the election of the Chairperson in the absence of chairpersons and Deputy Chairperson.
- The secretary performs the further duties laid upon him/her in Rules, and all other duties in the service of

the house ordered by the house or directed by the Chairperson.

- The secretary is responsible for preparing for each meeting an order paper showing all business for that meeting of which notice has been given.

Duties of Parliamentary Counsel

- He/she renders legal advice, either on his/her own notion or upon the request of the chairperson or a member on any legal issue, during the House proceedings.
- Subject to the direction of the chairperson ensures that the proceedings of the House are conducted in according with the law these Rules of Procedure.

Question & Motions in Ntlo ya Dikgosi

- Questions /motions asked shall conform to the Rules of Procedure, for example.
- Any members may address a question/motion to a minister relating to a public matter for which he/she is responsible, and either seeking information on such matter, or asking for official with regard to it.
- The Secretary then advises the Ministry to whom the question/motion to a minister relating to a public mater for which he/she is responsible, and either seeking information on such matter, or asking for official action with regard to it.

- No question can be asked without notice except as may be arranged with the Minister to whom it is addressed.
- Notice of a question/motion should be sent by a Member to reach the Secretary at last ten working days before commencement of the meeting.
- No question/motion shall seek information about a matter which is of its nature secret.
- No question/motion shall reflect on the of a court [sic] or be so drafted as to be likely to prejudice a case pending in a court of law.
- No question/motion shall be asking seeking information that can be found in inaccessible documents or ordinary works of reference.

Appendix 6: Favourability of traditional leaders compared to other institutions in South Sudan, 2011

Published with permission from International Republican Institute, *Survey of South Sudan Public Opinion, 6–27 September 2011*, www.iri.org.

For each institution and individual, please tell me whether you think very favorably, favorably, unfavorably or very unfavorably about them.

	Very Favorably	Favorably	Unfavorably	Very Unfavorably
The President	50%	32%	10%	4%
The Parliament	31%	40%	14%	6%
South Sudanese Armed Forces (former SPLA)	49%	32%	11%	5%
Your State's Governor	24%	32%	18%	20%
Women Politicians	36%	35%	13%	7%
Your State's Government	24%	36%	21%	12%
Opposition Political Parties	26%	33%	20%	11%
The Police	37%	35%	15%	9%
Judges and the Courts	32%	37%	15%	10%
Your Tribal Leaders	39%	39%	13%	5%
Foreign Government Officials	39%	38%	9%	4%
Foreign Nongovernmental Organizations	57%	28%	6%	4%
South Sudanese Who Lived in Sudan (North) and are Now Coming Back	46%	30%	12%	8%
South Sudanese Returning from Another Country	50%	34%	8%	5%

21

Appendix 7: Favourability of traditional leaders compared to other institutions in South Sudan, 2013

Published with permission from International Republican Institute, *Survey of South Sudan Public Opinion, 24 April –22 May 2013*, www.iri.org.

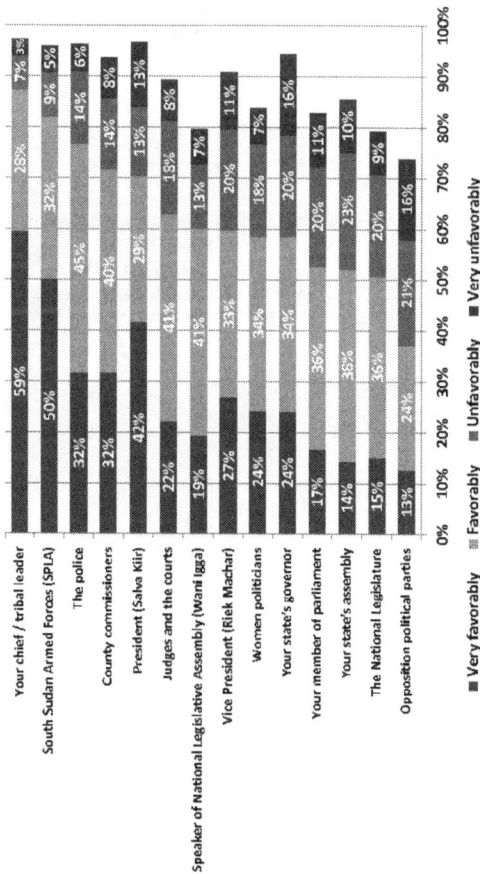

Now, I'm going to read you a list of institutions and individuals. For each one, please tell me whether you think very favorably, favorably, unfavorably or very unfavorably about them.

	Very favorably	Favorably	Unfavorably	Very unfavorably
Your chief / tribal leader	59%	28%	7%	3%
South Sudan Armed Forces (SPLA)	50%	32%	9%	5%
The police	32%	45%	14%	6%
County commissioners	32%	40%	14%	8%
President (Salva Kiir)	42%	29%	13%	13%
Judges and the courts	22%	41%	19%	8%
Speaker of National Legislative Assembly (Wani Igga)	19%	41%	13%	7%
Vice President (Riek Machar)	27%	33%	20%	11%
Women politicians	24%	34%	18%	7%
Your state's governor	24%	34%	20%	16%
Your member of parliament	17%	36%	20%	11%
Your state's assembly	14%	36%	23%	10%
The National Legislature	15%	36%	20%	9%
Opposition political parties	13%	24%	21%	16%

195

Appendix 8: Samples of certificates of endorsement of COTAL Act in Jonglei State and Upper Nile State in the Republic of South Sudan

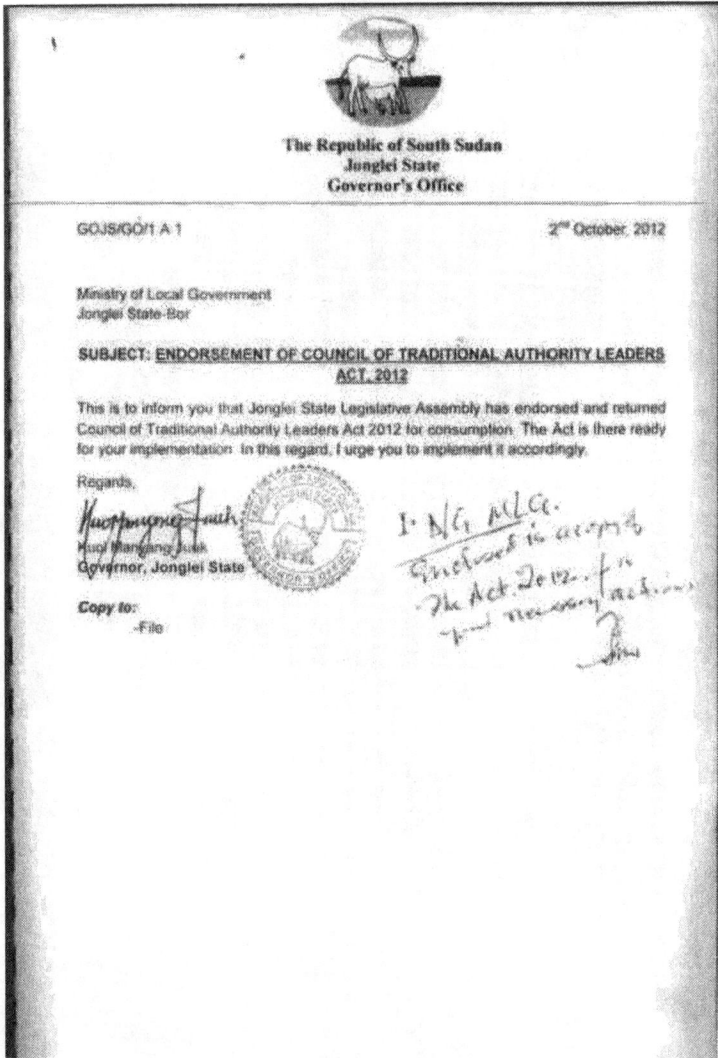

The Republic of South Sudan
Jonglei State
Governor's Office

GOJS/GO/1 A 1   2nd October, 2012

Ministry of Local Government
Jonglei State-Bor

SUBJECT: ENDORSEMENT OF COUNCIL OF TRADITIONAL AUTHORITY LEADERS ACT, 2012

This is to inform you that Jonglei State Legislative Assembly has endorsed and returned Council of Traditional Authority Leaders Act 2012 for consumption. The Act is there ready for your implementation. In this regard, I urge you to implement it accordingly.

Regards,

Governor, Jonglei State

Copy to:
-File

Acuil Malith Banggol

Government of Southern Sudan
Upper Nile State - Malakal
**Governor of Upper Nile State
Governor's Office**

Date: 23rd May 2011

No:

Assent of the Governor of Upper Nile State

In accordance with the certificate issued by the Acting Speaker of the Upper Nile State Legislative Assembly in passing the Bill of the COUNCIL OF TRADITIONAL AUTHORITY LEADERS, in their 33rd Sitting of the 1st Session of convention on Thursday, 31st of March 2011.

I, Maj. General Simon Kun Puoch, Governor of Upper Nile State, do hereby Assent to this Bill and sign into Law.

Made under my hand in Malakal, this Monday, the 23rd day of the Month of May in the year 2011.

Maj. General,
Simon Kun Puoch
Governor,
Upper Nile State
Malakal

ROLES OF TRADITIONAL AUTHORITY LEADERS

Appendix 9: President Kiir's views on federalism

Speech of His Excellency, the President of the Republic of South Sudan, Hon Salva Kiir Mayardit at the Official Consultative Conference for the Establishment of the Ministry of Federal Affairs, Republic of South Sudan

15 November 2016

The First Vice President, Minister for Federal Affairs, Ministers and Deputy Ministers of National Government, Ministers of State Governments, Undersecretaries, Ambassadors and representatives of Diplomatic missions and partners, ladies and gentlemen;

As the President of the Republic of South Sudan, I am committed to the principle and idea of federalism. The Government created 28 States and established 288 Counties, 27 Municipalities and 1 City Council in this spirit. We did this in response to the demand of the people of South Sudan, who wish to develop their communities, harness resources and govern themselves.

The hierarchy of the institutional framework for South Sudan, starts with the Boma, Payam, County, State and then National Government. I can assure you the commitment of the Government to the principle of federalism; we will ensure its implementation - where there is a will, there is a way, let us overcome the administrative and financial challenges we currently face, without losing sight of the guiding principle of federalism.

We believe that even in a multi-ethnic, geographically widespread and underdeveloped environment like that of South Sudan, federalism will catapult the country's development. Indeed federalism will bring Unity, and not division, we should remain united in our diversity and respect for our traditions and cultures. Federalism is not separation; it's the panacea to a united South Sudan.

In order to make the Federal system strong, Government will devolve more powers and resources to the lower level governments, that is States and Counties. The system of federalism will be run on democratic principles where there is transparency and accountability. The autonomy of lower level Governments is

198

protected by the Transitional Constitution and, that will be further reinforced in the constitution that is coming. In such a system, there will be minimal intervention from the National Government.

As the President, I would want to see that the main mandate of the Ministry of Federal Affairs ensures that the lower levels of government have the requisite capacities and are strengthened for the rapid development of South Sudan. The Ministry of Federal Affairs has the mandate to coordinate vertically and horizontally the activities of the various levels of Government. I strongly believe that federalism will bring lasting peace to South Sudan and provide for its rapid socio and economic development.

The Interim and Transitional Constitution, establishes institutions that are dealing with different aspects related to the Federal system of governance. The creation of the Ministry provides an opportunity to house all these plethora of institutions and bring them to work together harmoniously, complementing each other's efforts.

A good working relationship will be built between the Local Government Board whose mandate is defined in the Local Government Act 2009, and the Ministry of Federal Affairs. The mandate the Ministry of Federal Affairs is to create an equivalent of the Local Government Board for building of the capacity of the states and for coordination. The Ministry of Federal Affairs will oversee the 28 States and ensure they are functional and performing so as to serve the people of South Sudan.

I would like to challenge the people of South Sudan not to get bogged down by terminology and endless debates of our governmental system - but to appreciate that we have selected a devolved governmental system and that it is time to make it work.

I want to wish the participants of this important workshop successful deliberations as they breathe life into the Ministry of federal Affairs. I am also calling upon the development community to support the Government of South Sudan as it implements the federal system of government.

Appendix 10: Study/familiarisation tour of traditional leaders from the Republic of South Sudan to South Africa, Botswana and Ghana

13 January – 01 February 2013

1   *Hon.* Tor Deng MAWIEN BAK, Presidential Advisor on Decentralisation and Intergovernmental Linkages

2   Garang AKOK, Office Manager of the Presidential Advisor on Decentralisation and Intergovernmental Linkages

3   *Hon.* James Lual DENG KUEL, Chairperson of Committee for Foreign Affairs and International Cooperation, National Legislative Assembly

4   *Hon.* John MASUA MADANZA, Chairperson of Committee for Decentralized Governance and State Affairs, National Legislature, Council of States

5   *P/Chief* Agol Ayuel Adway AGOL, Chairperson of COTAL Upper Nile

6   *Matat* Alfonse Legge Loku TOMBE, Chairperson of COTAL Central Equatoria

7   *Bakindo* (King) Wilson Peni Rikito GBUDUE, King of Zande

8   *Nyiiya* (King) Akwai Agada AKWAI, King of Anyuak

9   *P/Chief* Achien Achien YOR, Paramount Chief of Northern Bahr El Ghazal

10 *Gbia* (P/Chief) Angelo Bagari Umgbanga UKOVO, Paramount Chief of Western Bahr El Ghazal

11 *P/Chief* David Mangar Nhial KON, Paramount Chief of Lakes State

12   *P/Chief* Manoon Ater Guot CHOL, Executive Chief of Warrap

13   Del Rumdit DENG, Director General of Local Government and Traditional Authorities, Local Government Board, Office of the President

14   James Alala DENG, President of Court of Appeal Greater Bahr El Ghazal, Judiciary

15   Adam Abwol Kiir DENG, Legal Counsel, Ministry of Justice

16   Ms Jackline Novello Nailock TAMOT, Director for Gender, Ministry of Gender, Child and Social Welfare

17   Ms Margret Akon Isaiah MAJOK, Gender Focal Point, Ministry of Gender, Child and Social Welfare

18   Acuil Malith BANGGOL, Gurtong Trust Board Member

19   Toby COLLINS, Sudan Tribune

20   Oliver HUMBEL, Human Security Advisor, Federal Department of Foreign Affairs, Switzerland

21   Kwesi Kwaa PRAH, Tour Leader, Professor, Centre for Advanced Studies on African Society (CASAS)

REFERENCES

Bass, Bernard M. & Rinald E. Riggio (2006), *Transformational Leadership* (2nd edn), Mahwah New Jersey, USA: Lawrence Erlbaum Associates.

Bolman, Lee G. & Terrence E. Deal (2003), *Reframing Organizations-Artistry, Choice and Leadership* (3rd edn), San Francisco: Jossey-Bass, A Wiley Imprint

Charmatz, Kathy (2006), *Constructing Grounded Theory*, Thousand Oaks/London/New Delhi: SAGE Publications.

Covey Stephen R. (2004), *The 8th Habit: From Effectiveness to Greatness,* New York, USA: Simon & Schuster.

Creswell, John W. (2009), *Research Design: Qualitative, Quantitative and Mixed Approaches* (3rd edn), Thousand Oaks/London/New Delhi: SAGE Publications.

Deng, Lual A. (2013), *The Power of Creative Reasoning*, Bloomington: iUniverse.

Erickson, Frederick (1986), Qualitative Methods in Research on Teaching, in Merlin C. Wittrock (ed.) *Handbook of Research on Teaching* (3rd edn) New York, USA: Macmillan, 119–161.

Flamholtz, Eric & Yvonne Randle (2008), *Leading Strategic Change, Bridging the Theory and Practice,* Cambridge, UK/New York: Cambridge University Press.

Gaventa, John & Camilo Valderrama (1999), *Participation, Citizenship and Local Governance,* Background note prepared for workshop on "Strengthening Participation in Local Governance", Institute of Development Studies, 21–24 June 1999, http://www.uv.es/~fernandm/Gaventa,%20Valderrama.pdf, accessed 15 June 2016.

Government of Southern Sudan (2009), *Laws of Southern Sudan, the Local Government Act, 2009,* Juba, Southern Sudan: Ministry of Justice.

Hames, Richard David (2007), *The Five Literacies of Global Leadership: What Authentic Leaders Know and You Need to Find Out,* San Francisco: Jossey-Bass, A Wiley Imprint.

Hoehne, Markus S. (2008), *Traditional Authorities and Local Government in Southern Sudan,* Max Planck Institute for Social Anthropology, Halle/Saale, Germany, consultancy report for the World Bank, Washington, USA.

Igga, Wani (2010), *South Sudan, Discovering Our Roots,* Kampala, Uganda: Roberts & Brothers.

Institute for Democratic Governance (2010) *Ghana's Traditional Authorities in Governance and Development,* Accra, Ghana: Institute for Democratic Governance.

Intergovernmental Authority on Development (2015), *Agreement on the Resolution of the Conflict in the Republic of South Sudan, Addis Ababa, Ethiopia, Addis Ababa, Ethiopia, 17 August 2015,* https://drive.google.com/file/d/0B5FAwdVtt-

gCelBQZVAxbjhUc1FmSHo3VnNaT09Ldm1GNEh
z/view, accessed 15 June 2016.

Johari, J. C. (2009), *Principles of Modern Political Science,* New Delhi: Sterling Publishers.

Kenyi, Christopher (2012), *Kajokeji Strategic Development Plan,* Kajokeji and Juba: Kajokeji Development Trust.

Koller, Arnold et al. (2010), *Principles of Federalism. Guidelines for Good Federal Practices – a Swiss contribution,* Baden-Baden: Nomos Verlag; Zurich: Dike Verlag.

Kuol, Kuol Deng-Abot (2008), *An Investigation of the Roles of Traditional Leaders in The Liberation Struggle in Southern Sudan From 1983–2004,* MA Dissertation, University of Fort Hare, Republic of South Africa, http:// contentpro.seals.ac.za/ iii/cpro/app?id=5348277643167352&itemId=100125 6&lang=eng&service=blob&suite=def, accessed 15 June 2016.

Lee, Robert J. & Sara N. King (2001), *Discovering the Leaders in You, A Guide to Realizing Your, Personal Leadership Potentials,* San Francisco: John Wiley & Sons.

Madut-Arop, Arop (2012), *The Genesis of Political Consciousness in South Sudan,* Charleston, SC, USA: Createspace.

Malok, Elija (2009), *The Southern Sudan – Struggle for Liberty,* Nairobi, Kenya: Kenway Publications.

Mayen, David D. 2013. *House of War: Civil War and State Failure in Africa.* N.p.:Lambert Academic Publishing.

Moyo, Dambisa (2010), *Dead Aid: Why Aid Is Not Working and How There Is a Better Way for Africa*, New York: Farrar, Straus and Giroux.

Okoth-Ogendo, H. W. O. (2007), *Resolving the Land Question in Southern Sudan*, (PhD) A paper prepared for Norwegian People's Aid's Land Policy Development Work in Southern Sudan, Norwegian People's Aid, Southern Sudan (unpublished report).

Organization of African Unity (1981), *African (Banjul) Charter on Human and Peoples' Rights*, eighteenth Assembly of Heads of State and Government, http://www.achpr.org/files/instruments/achpr/banjul_charter.pdf, accessed 15 June 2016.

Republic of Botswana (n.d.), *Powers and Functions Ntlo ye Dikgosi*, Gaborone, Botswana: Parliament of Botswana.

Republic of Botswana (n.d.), *Duties and the House Business*, Gaborone, Botswana: Parliament of Botswana.

Republic of South Sudan (2009), *Laws of the Republic Of South Sudan, Local Government Act (LGA) 2009*, Juba, South Sudan: Ministry of Justice.

Republic of South Sudan (2011), *Laws of the Republic Of South Sudan, The Transitional Constitution, 2011*, Juba, South Sudan: Ministry of Justice.

Santschi, Martina (2010), *Chiefs, State-Building, and Development in Independent South Sudan*, Evidence for Policy Series, Regional edition Horn of Africa, No. 5, Berhanu Debele (ed.). Addis Ababa, Ethiopia: NCCR North–South.

Sharma, Kehav C. (2010), *Role of Traditional Structures in Local Governance for Local Development – The Case of Botswana,* Prepared for Community Empowerment and Social Inclusion Program (CESI), World Bank Institute, World Bank, Washington, USA.

Simonse, Simon and Eisei Kuirmoto (eds) (2011), *Engaging Monyomiji, Bridging the Governance Gap in East Bank Equatoria, Proceedings of the Conference 26–28 November 2009, Torit,* Nairobi, Kenya: Pax Christi Horn of Africa.

Simonsen, Peggy (1997), *Promoting Development Culture in Your Organization: Using Career Development as a Change Agent,* Palo Alto, California, USA: Davis Black Publishing.

Strauss, Anselm & Juliet M. Corbin (2007), *Basics of qualitative research: Techniques and Procedures for Developing Grounded Theory,* Thousand Oaks, CA: Sage Publications.

Sudan People's Liberation Movement Economic Commission (2004), *SPLM Strategic Framework for War-to-Peace Transition,* New Site, Kapoeta County, https://paanluelwel.com/2012/03/01/splm-strategic-framework-for-war-to-peace-transition-2004/, accessed 15 June 2016.

Sudan People's Liberation Movement (2008) *Constitution of the SPLM 2008,* http://www.splmtoday.com/index.php/about/constitution-of-the-splm, accessed 15 June 2016.

Sudan People's Liberation Movement (2008), *Manifesto of the SPLM 2008,* http://www.

splmtoday.com/docs/SPLM%20docs/2008%20The% 20Manifesto%20of%20the%20SPLM.pdf, accessed 15 June 2016.

Tagore, Rabindranath, (1915), 'Unity in Diversity', in Sirdar Ikbal Ali Shah (1984 [1933]), The *Oriental Caravan*, London, UK: Darf Publishers.

Tier, Akolda M. & Abraham M. Dhal (2005), *Inter-communal Conflict in Sudan: Causes, Resolution Mechanisms and Transformation. 3, A case study of the Dinka–Nuer Conflict*, Omdurman: Ahfad University for Women.

Wassara, Samson S. (2007), *Traditional Mechanisms of Conflict Resolution in South Sudan*, Bergdorf Foundation for Peace Support, https://villierspark.org.uk/wp-content/uploads/2014/ 09/0979-Wassara-2007-Traditional-Mechanisms-of-CR-in-South-Sudan.pdf, accessed 15 June 2016.

Yom, Peter Atem (2008), *Dinka Relationship With Political Governments In North Sudan in Modern History (1504–1956)*. Khartoum Sudan, University of el Nilein. Dissertation for partial fulfilment of Master's Degree in History. Unpublished, in Arabic.

Zaninotto, Claudio (2011), *When two elephants are fighting... it's the grass that suffers*, n.: Associazione Amici di Lino Poisa (www.associazioneanthropos.it).